DEAR GOD

I CAN'T DO ME
WITHOUT YOU

Ashley Ertilien

Publisher: Luminous Publishing
www.luminouspublishing.com
For bulk orders or other inquiries, email:
info@luminouspublishing.com

TABLE OF CONTENTS

PREFACE

I originally wanted to title this book *Introverts vs. God——The intrinsic battle between introverted believers and the omnipotence of God.* But as time went on, only one phrase came to mind when I thought of all God had brought me through which is Dear God, I can't do me without You. Symbolically, the title of this book sounds like the beginning of a letter because, while writing, I was in constant communication with God like never before. Our communication was not just in prayer but in conversation. He is my best friend and like best friends, I have a lot to tell Him, and I know He always has something to share with me.

I also didn't go with the original title because introversion turned out to be one chapter of my life. My introverted characteristics were never meant to take over the entire conversation. So what you will read on the following pages is the culmination of what took place when God freed me from the chains I had cuffed to my mind. There was literally no way I could do me, achieve my goals, and do this thing called life to the fullest, in its truest sense, without Him.

I hope and pray that as you read and flip through the pages of this book, something within you will be awakened and spurred into action immediately. Do not wait for tomorrow to get what you have the vision to plant today. Take advantage of the breath in your lungs.

Dear God,

I can't do me without You.

CHAPTER 1:

PURPOSE, PLANS, & PURSUIT

Dear God,

This isn't me...speaking to people. It is one thing to have a conversation with friends and family and another to teach little kids on Sunday morning. But to speak to a crowd of people I don't know...place myself at center stage to be seen and to be heard...nah, that's not me. I don't have the confidence, ability, or personality to motivate and inspire a group of people I am not familiar with. Why can't I just be by myself and do me? Writing is my thing but speaking in crowds is a no-no. You know this. I'm an introvert, remember? That's how you made me.

....

I learned very quickly I could not serve God by remaining tethered to the introverted characteristics I had always been bound to. The girl who told God He had made her an introvert was the same girl now saying I cannot serve God and plead my case as an introvert. Why? Because it is a lie that I am to live according to the pieces that make me and not according to the vision God predestined me for. The girl who claimed to be an introvert didn't realize that walking according to the world's limited understanding was like placing foggy glasses on the all-powerful God or beholding the all-powerful God with foggy glasses. You see, the world told me I was limited. And I believed them. I bought into who I was supposed to be by depending on my innate characteristics. As a result, I limited God's hand in my life. I was deeply focused on me, my abilities, and supposed lack thereof. I concentrated on my discomfort, which in turn hindered me from walking in my purpose. I was so willing to accept what the world said about me that I never considered the living God who was in me. I never once thought about how the almighty God gracefully exchanges our weaknesses for His strength.

That being said, the lie is not that I never had introverted tendencies because I am introverted by nature. The lie is that I had to live according to that nature. I discovered I did not have to, and it was a marvelous revelation. See, 2 Timothy 1:7 empowers us: "For the Spirit God gave us does not make us timid, but gives us power, love, and self-discipline."

Whenever I encounter a new obstacle whether internal or external, I am reminded of Romans 12:1, which encourages us to "Offer your bodies as a living sacrifice, holy and pleasing to God—this is your true and proper worship." Above all, our weaknesses play no part in the end result. Instead, we are confident in what Philippians 4:13 reminds us: "I can do all things through Christ who strengthens me."

Speaking of doing all things through Christ, He has given each of us a mission to fulfill our purpose. Yes, we all have specific assignments, but we also have one that we share.

We learn in John 20:1-2 and 11-16 that on the third day after Christ died, Mary and Mary Magdalene went to Jesus' tomb to wrap Him in new oil and linen. However, when they got there, they found an overturned stone and an empty tomb. As promised, it was the third day since his death and Jesus was not there. After encountering an angel who confirmed this, the ladies came face-to-face with Jesus on their way back to the disciples. Jesus instructed the women to tell the disciples to meet Him in Galilee. It is during this meeting, after He had died and resurrected, that He gave the disciples their mission:

> *Therefore go and make disciples of all nations, baptizing them in the name of the Father and of the Son and of the Holy Spirit, and teaching them to obey everything I have commanded you.*
> (Matthew 28:19-20, NIV)

The same instruction is recorded again in Mark 16:15-18. Please understand that this mission is not solely for the disciples who stood on that mountain in Galilee with Jesus. The weight of the mission meant that if the disciples obeyed, then we, as believers of Christ, would be included in that assignment. It is not simply a question of conversion but one of discipleship, teaching, modeling, and encouraging others to grow the pack. Our keyword here is "Go!"

As kids riding in my parent's car, every time the light turned green, my siblings and I would yell "Go!" We would yell, not because our parents didn't notice the stoplight turn green, but because we were excited to get to our destination. We knew we had all the resources (the car, gas, driver) we needed for the journey and our end goal which was to get the destination. In the same way, my friends, the light is green, and God says, "Go!" For too long I let my introvert-like characteristics stop me from reaching my destination. But that ends here. There is no reason to hold up traffic or pull over. I have to trust I have everything I need to live a life that is pleasing to God. I am not lacking and neither are you (2 Peter 1:3).

It feels good to have a mission. It feels good to feel like we have a reason for being, to know that our lives matter, and we can make an impact, be it one-to-one, generational, or world-wide. But like any mission, tools and resources are necessary. You may be wondering, well what does this look like? Where can we find the tools?

The tools are our gifts. In Ephesians 4:11-12 and 1 Corinthians 12:1-10, we learn the following of Jesus: "When he ascended on high, he took many captives and gave gifts to his people." We also learn the gifts given to us by His Spirit are "given for the common good." My favorite part of these passages is how God debunks the lie the Enemy would try to convince you of even now as you read this chapter. God said, "All these are the work of one and the same Spirit, and he distributes them to each, just as he determines." The Holy Spirit distributes gifts to each of us. None of our tool bags are empty, so let's open them up and discover what they're filled with and let's practice using those tools so we can develop our expertise.

In Matthew 25:14-30, we will discover the story of the Master who gave three servants a different number of talents. One servant received five, another two, and the last received one talent. The servants with two and five talents went out and invested them hoping they would multiply. What does this look like in our lives? We know that God's Spirit gave each of us gifts and talents as He determined. Please note that different translations of this passage use the words "talents" and "silver" interchangeably as "talents" in this time period referred to monetary measurement. Due to the version of Scripture being used and the example set above, we will continue to use the word "talent."

Some of us may have five talents, two talents, or just one. Let's say, for example, we are gifted in faith, wisdom, and teaching. We know God, our Master, has given us these gifts. Have we invested in them? How? Have we used our faith to inspire faith in others? Have we used our wisdom to avoid the Enemy's traps or help others grow? Have we held our tongues from sharing knowledge that could change generational legacies? What have we done to multiply the talents God has given us? Has there been a return on our Master's investment?

The point is that we are tasked to go out and make a return on God's investment in us. The best part is that when we go out with these talents, we produce and multiply by His power, not our own. What about the servant who received only one talent? Well, that servant who was worried about the risk of investing and losing his one talent still returned empty-handed.

Friend, in a world where we gamble and take risks, we cannot guarantee the outcomes. We don't lose because we run out of luck. We lose because we place our faith in a dying world. However, when we take this same gamble with our one talent in Christ, the risk no longer exists because, in Christ, there is only life. One talent is necessary and can make a big difference. Think about it. We have one head; yet, it controls so much of how we operate. We have one heart that pumps blood to every corner of our bodies and allows every organ to function correctly. We have one stomach, which has the capacity to expand and shrink, allocate nutrients, bind waste, fill us up, and let us know when we've had enough. The one talent matters.

Your presence, the way you encourage those around you, your knowledge, way of organizing, and your smile—all of these and more can generate returns on God's investment in you. Do not discount the gifts placed in your hands simply because they do not look like everyone else's. Be a faithful steward of what has been given to you. Pursue purpose and live on purpose. I want to emphasize we must continue to move one step after another. We can no longer sit back and wait for something to come to us. The pursuit of our mission requires faith. Faith is believing and moving even when we cannot see the final destination. Make a return on the Father's investment in you. You have the mission and you have the tools. There is no way you can lose.

Where would I be had I allowed my fear, introverted characteristics, and the exposure of my weaknesses to be the reason I refused to make a return on God's investment in me?

I want to encourage you to read Ephesians Chapter 4 and 1 Corinthians Chapter 12 in their entirety. Afterward, create a list of your gifts. This list does not need to be made up of only spiritual gifts but a reflection of what you feel you are good at or possibly an expert in. Test your list of gifts against these two questions:

1. Does this gift connect me directly and/or indirectly with people?

2. Is this gift something I do well? Would the fruit produced be multiplied if I gave it to God?

We can pose lots of other questions to test this list of gifts. Questions like: is this something I could see myself doing for the long term? Do I like this gift of mine? Am I good at making use of this gift?

But as great as these questions are to reflect on, they are based on emotions and cannot be the baseline for what gifts you believe the Spirit allocated to you.

Let's look at the story of Moses. He was known for being a leader. A leader is an example or model for others to imitate or follow. When we think of the phrase "Follow the leader" from our elementary school days, the leader always stood in the front and whatever he or she did we had to copy. A leader not only has to lead by example but also be able to speak and influence a single person or a body of people. Let's assume Moses created his list and on it, he has "Leader," not necessarily because he really believes this, but he has been called a leader by his friends and family all his life. Now, let's say he tests this against the set of questions I just mentioned above.

I am a leader. Is this something I could see myself doing for the long term? *No, because I'm an outsider and no one cares what I have to say.*

I am a leader. Do I like this gift of mine? *No, because it puts me in high-pressure situations, wherein I may have to advocate for a group of people when I could have just been doing me by myself.*

I am a leader. Am I good at making use of this gift? *No, I have a stuttering problem. Period.*

Now, let's test them against the two previous questions I asked you to test your list against, while still using Moses as an example.

I am a leader. Does this gift connect me directly and/or indirectly with people? *Yes, it connects me directly with people.*

I am a leader. If this gift is something I do well, would the fruit produced be multiplied if I gave it to God? *Yes, I thought it was because I was raised in Pharaoh's house, but people listen when I speak and they watch my every move.*

So why ask if this gift connects us directly and/or indirectly with people? Because we know that God has called us to go out and make disciples. You can't do that if your gift does not connect you in some way with people. Some of us are asked to literally go out and evangelize by testimony. Still, God can use us through our sermons, books, and even our social media accounts to reach out to people. I pose the second question because of what the scripture says in Luke 5:4 and John 21:6. Peter was a fisherman by profession, which means he must have been good at what he does. But one early morning, he found he couldn't catch any fish. Then Jesus Christ instructed him to throw his net over to the right side, and Peter collected so much fish that his boat began to sink. When we give our gifts to God, be obedient to what He asks us to do, and how He instructs us to use them, the fruit will multiply beyond our capacity. This is overflow.

Imagine what would have happened if Moses wasn't obedient to the call (Exodus 3:10). What if Joseph was over being wrongly accused and allowed his frustration to stop him from saving his countrymen from famine (Genesis 41:28-36)? Walking in obedience and our purpose is less about us and more about God's glory and the impact our obedience will have on His people for generations to come. Despite everything, Moses and Joseph are great examples of walking in their purpose according to God's plan. God never said it would be easy. But neither is life. Of the two ways to live your life: with God or without God, only one will bring joy and satisfaction even in the middle of trial and tribulation.

Let It Go

We struggle with sin. For some of us it isn't that we aren't aware of our responsibility to go out and make disciples neither is it that we aren't aware of the gifts in our tool bags. Some of us stay silent and away from the light because we want to get right first. Like I said we struggle with sin. But knowing that Jesus already washed us clean is why salvation is so freeing. Jesus isn't just our Lord; He is our Savior. The two cannot be separated. At times we look to God as Lord and scary Commander but like any father who wants his children to come to him and admit a mistake, God our Father wants us to know we can find forgiveness and help in Him. We cannot overcome sin by ourselves.

In the first place, we find sin tempting because it temporarily satiates what we perceive to be a need or a desire. We understand sin is dangerous because of its ability to overpower our desire to do right. We acknowledge that in the moment of temptation, sin's intangible force subdues our efforts to do better. This is most prominent when we try to overcome sin by ourselves and when we try to do things without the power of the Holy Spirit. This is where Jesus our Savior and God our loving Father steps in. God can help pull us out of those cycles we keep getting ourselves stuck in. It is by the blood that we can know chains are loosed not by our will.

Consider this instance: today you decided to change your lifestyle, so you can be happy about what you see in the mirror. Without pausing to create a grocery list, or conduct research, or consult God you drive over to the grocery store. You're excited! But before you can make it to the register with your basket full of items, you walk by a strategically placed array of cookies. Wow! They're on sale. You find it difficult to overlook the mouthwatering offer and make quick and biased calculations in your mind to justify buying them. It isn't until you're unloading your groceries in your kitchen that you realize your mistake. How are you going to train yourself up for healthy living with fresh temptation at the ready? It's not your fault. You like sweets and so of course you wanted to buy them. I can't count the number of times I got stuck in this exact predicament. Trial after trial I had to learn that the only way out was to let God in.

Jesus is Lord and Savior at all times. He is here to save us in the good, the bad, and the mundane. Do not misunderstand me. It is easier said than done, no matter your predicament. Sometimes lost in the middle of my own mess, I feel too far gone to go and ask for help. When I do finally build up the courage to tilt my head up and ask God to take over, I'm reminded that it is He who brings beauty from ashes

(Isaiah 61:1-3). But even when life is manageable, I forget to seek his direction. It's seems that as long as the wind isn't blowing, and my boat isn't rocking I think it isn't necessary to ask for help.

Maybe you've felt the same way at times? Here's what I've learned. Just because it doesn't look like I need saving, doesn't mean there isn't a war waging beneath the surface, waiting for the perfect opportunity to catch me off guard and capsize the whole boat. You and I can't always be aware of what goes on around us. We need saving even before we see the next obstacle formed against us. Don't miss understand me. I'm not into walking around like a victim my whole life. I am about acknowledging my weaknesses and partnering with someone who is strong where I'm not. In any case, if I had to choose teams, it would be me and God. I think sometimes we choose not to partner with God because we think he takes too long to respond. This is why patience is key. We can't let impatience be the reason we walk out on God. For example, in Daniel 10, Daniel learns of the war that had been waging in the heavenly realms. This war had delayed God's response to his prayer for three weeks. But he would not have known had it not been made known to him, because from what he could see, all was quiet. There was no storm. In fact, he could have assumed that maybe God was "too busy to hear him." But the truth is God is still working on our behalf in the quiet. Let's see what happens when life is better than quiet.

When we look at the story of the rich young ruler in Matthew 19:16-23, we discover that his life was about as good as it could get. He had all the material things every man desires. He obeyed the laws and was a good person. One day, he approached Jesus and asked Him what a guy had to do to have eternal life. Makes sense, right? He had everything he could ever want or need and all that was left was to be able to live forever and enjoy these rewards. Jesus told the rich man he would have to sell all his possessions, give the money to the poor, and follow Him. Hearing that he would have to give his riches to the poor, the man was unsettled and walked away. What is this story about? I can tell you it is about more than a rich man giving to the poor. When life is looking good, sometimes we ask Jesus a simple question, "What more can I do to serve you?" Somehow, we're never ready for His response.

Jesus told the rich, young ruler to do something that perhaps many of us would find difficult to do. Jesus asked the rich man to strip himself of the things that gave him a sense of security and control. But we can't stop there. After selling his riches and giving the proceeds to the poor, he would then have to leave the space he had grown familiar with to follow Jesus. This tells me that God wants us to be willing to relinquish the things and spaces that are familiar and be in willing to trust Him.

Speaking for myself, it gets easier to let go of things when it becomes a habit. Practice giving now no matter how small and be willing to be stretched in your giving. This doesn't mean you have to be poor to be a follower of Jesus Christ. In fact, I believe the opposite. I think learning to trust God over and over again is a reminder to remain humble. If life were always easy, how easy would it be to forget our God who brought us to those blessings. My point is whether life is unpredictable but staying at the feet of Jesus is our only guarantee. So what if our faith means we will rock the boat that is our lives? As written in Matthew 6:33, "Seek first the kingdom of God and His righteousness, and all these things shall be added to you." Do rich people take their assets with them when they die? Of course not! They enter eternity empty-handed. However, despite the socio-economic status of those who follow Christ, when we die, we gain everything. We leave our earthly assets behind and receive eternal life as heirs in God's kingdom.

If you were the rich man in this story and you had walked away from Jesus because you didn't want to relinquish all you had, what would you do if thieves came in the night and took it away from you anyway? Would you stay in your now empty house or would you run after Jesus? Would you run after Jesus realizing the fragility of earthly possessions? Would you pursue Him understanding that the fruit of your labor is not of more value than what God is offering you for free? Would you give God permission to rock your boat and increase your faith as He brings you to the promised land?

Sometimes we make decisions based on what we can see and based on the wisdom of the world. But the wisdom of the world is foolishness to God. Scripture makes this clear in 1 Corinthians 3:19.

In Jeremiah 29:11, God said, "For I know the plans I have for you...plans to prosper you and not to harm you, plans to give you hope and a future."

God always wants the best for His children. When we live according to our will and not His, we risk forfeiting the blessings, protection, and other benefits that come with walking with Him. For example, when our parents tell us to do well in school, it is because they want us to have a better future. At the time, we may not understand. Perhaps, we ignore this command. What our parents see is how good grades can lead to stable finances and access to whatever we desire in adulthood. All we see is our desire to hang out with friends and live our best lives according to the moment. Sometimes we learn this lesson too late. Our friends and siblings go to schools that have more opportunities, and we end up having to work twice as hard to make up for our mess. In the same way, the sooner we acquiesce to God's plans for our lives, the more assured we will be in knowing that everything will work out for our good even in the middle of the storm. I don't know about you, but I'm giving God permission to rock my boat. I won't pretend that at times I won't be holding on to the edge of the boat, praying that I stay in it. Still, I'd rather live standing on faith then to have the illusion of solid ground beneath my feet.

To bring this full circle, bless the Lord for how He created you, introvert or extrovert, comedian or sarcastic, tall or short. He did it on purpose. It is for God's glory that introverts would go outside their comfort zones and do the things that are the opposite of their strengths. It is for God's glory that short people would reach higher to do what people their height typically wouldn't do. God shows up in our weaknesses so He can get the glory. It's your turn to show up and see what God wants to do through you. But God can only do this if you make Him Lord and Savior of your life.

God is good and faithful through our every misstep and outright decision to disobey Him. I implore you to repent and to give thanks for His grace and mercy. Let us pursue Him and the desires of His heart. Let us run after our purpose in the way He designed it when He thought of us before we were created. Let us walk hand in hand with our Lord and Savior. He'll take care of the transformation along the way. May we know that every mountain was meant to strengthen us and every valley to humble us. Most importantly, let us do this together. We weren't meant to go through life alone. As your sister in Christ, I want to "go" with you. It can feel like a long way to heaven, but a little laughter, encouragement, and friendly competition always makes the time go by quickly. Get ready for the craziest ride of your life where your weakness is your greatest strength in God's hands.

CHAPTER 2:

EMPTINESS

Dear God,

How are You? Thank You for this day. I will rejoice and be glad in it. Thank You for this opportunity to walk with You, worship You, speak to You, and hear from You.

Just a moment ago, I told You I was hungry. I asked if I could eat on my lunch break today. You said, "No." I can't lie; at that moment, I thought maybe I was talking to myself. Maybe I was trying to challenge myself and see just how far I was willing to go. But your Word says that my works do nothing, so that can't be it. Alright then, no to food it is.

....

In the first few moments of stepping out the door into the cold wind, hungry and alone, God took the time to tell me something so powerful, yet, so sweet.

God told me, *"Emptiness is an opportunity to be filled by Me."*

Knock Knock

Let's look at John's three letters in Revelation Chapter 3. One of them was to a church in Sardis, another to a church in Philadelphia, and the third letter to a church in Laodicea. John begins each letter by addressing the church and informs them that the contents of the letters were written for their specific situation.

We will be focusing on the third letter written to the church in Laodicea. They received the revelation that Jesus was about to spit them out of His mouth. You're probably shocked and wondering why Jesus would want to spit anything out of His mouth.

Let's consider this example: I buy a bowl of ice-cream on a hot summer day. Then, I try my best to both devour and savor my bowl of ice-cream as efficiently as possible. Why? Because I know that as soon as it melts into a lukewarm milkshake, I'll no longer enjoy its taste. In the same way, Jesus does not like it when we are lukewarm, neither hot nor cold, for Him or against Him (Revelation 3:16). Jesus tells the members of the church in Laodicea to repent, explaining that He rebukes and disciplines those He loves (Revelations 3:19). Desiring that the church of Laodicea would turn from their ways, Jesus invites them saying, "Here I am! I stand at the door and knock. If anyone hears my voice and opens the door, I will come in and eat with him, and he with me."

Emptiness is an opportunity to be filled by God. What causes us to go from hot to lukewarm? One day, we're on fire for Jesus and then the next day, we're looking for something else, someone else to fill us up.

We are guilty of being lukewarm. Even as you read this book, you can probably think of one or more areas where you aren't all in with Jesus. We've got one foot in the church and the other led by our flesh. We pray for forgiveness all the while planning out the details of our next spiritual rebellion. Whether we stand in the shadows at night or in our offices during the day, our lights are supposed to shine, and our lifestyles should glorify God. We're excited to tell everyone we are Christians. But, we refuse to confront the areas in our lives where we fall short and can lean on God's power to overcome. I'm not talking about perfection; rather, I'm talking about progress, which requires that we acknowledge our missteps and correct them. Thank You God for ordering our steps so that even when we stumble, we do not fall (Psalm 37:23-24).

Lukewarm living is usually connected to a disordered life or spirit. When we are intentional about our relationship with God in the same way that we are intentional about hitting up our friends to update them on the crazy thing that happen at work, we give God's Spirit access to order our steps. On the other hand, when it isn't God's Spirit passing on instruction, it means our flesh is leading us. Being led by our flesh is a sure way to run out of the power we need to keep doing not just everyday things but even big, impossible God things. Matthew 6:33 tells us to seek God first and He will take care of the rest of our desires.

This suggests that going after our desires without God could be detrimental and possibly unsatisfying. But also, if all I have to do is get in relationship with God why would I want to tire myself chasing after anything less?

Being half in for Jesus is the same as being against Him altogether. You can't ride a bike and a skateboard at the same time. You'll end up either riding the bike with an uncomfortable skateboard in one hand or you'll ride the skateboard while you drag the bike along. It just doesn't make sense to try to ride two different vehicles to get to your destination. But this is what we look like when we want just a little bit of Jesus and a little bit of whatever our flesh desires. Not to mention the concentration is takes to be moving up a hill with a bike and a skateboard. Who knows how long it'll take you to get to the top of the hill? If you're not looking to be the person riding a bike and a skateboard up a hill, then I encourage you to make a decision. Are you in or are you out?

In our lukewarm state, we will always run on empty even when the gas tank says full. I refer to this as lukewarm because we look to our desires to be the compass that directs us to our next meal, instead of fixing our eyes on the cross that directs us to the Living Water. Kirk Franklin and Rodney Jerkins remind us of the words written in Revelation 7:16, which say that in Jesus, we shall hunger no more neither shall we thirst anymore (*Revolution*, The Nu Nation Project, 1998).

Jesus wanting to spit what is lukewarm out from His mouth tells how nothing is pleasing about dead men walking. In Luke 6:46, Jesus said, "Why do you call me, 'Lord, Lord,' and do not do what I say?" Ouch! How many of us are guilty of this? I know I am. So many times, God has instructed us to do or to turn away from something. We hear Him; we understand, but we do not obey.

Over and over again, Jesus said, "Here I am! I stand at the door and knock. If anyone hears my voice and opens the door, I will come in and eat with him, and he with me." God is knocking on our doors. He desires to fill those hungry and empty places. I understand you feel lonely, unworthy, way past the point of no return, unqualified, undesirable, forgettable, too small, or too big. I get it. But it's all a lie. Drown out the noise and look up to Jesus.

Sometimes while I'm driving, the point comes when there seems to be too much noise around me. I tell everyone to be quiet so I can see where I'm going. Yeah, that's right. It makes no sense but as soon as there is silence in the car, my vision gradually clears and so do my thoughts. I can distinguish safety from danger and arrive at my destination without interruption. In the same way, I'm asking you to silence the noise. Step away from the friends for a moment. Step away from the work for a moment. Step away from the alcohol and the things that take up the space God wants to replace.

You're hungry and you feel empty, Jesus knows this and wants to fill you up. So, go to the door.

Knock knock.
Who's there?

....

Emptiness is an opportunity to be filled by God. It is also a reminder that we are running low on Him. How did Erica Campbell put it in her song? I need just a little more Jesus. Google defines emptiness as the state of containing nothing; the quality of lacking meaning or sincerity; meaninglessness.

When We Give the World a Chance
Consider this example of emptiness. Those of us who have vehicles know that just because we filled our cars up with gas two weeks ago doesn't mean they will remain full after two weeks. In fact, when we enter our cars, our eyes automatically measure the amount of gas remaining in the tank. Some of us will see the pointer touching

the halfway point and that's enough of a warning to go and fill it up again. For others, that halfway mark doesn't mean half empty but half-full. As nice as that sounds, half-full still means half-empty. Half-empty may not be enough to get you to your destination and back. Soon, your car will warn you to fill it up.

Just like a gas tank, our spiritual lives need to be fed and refueled consistently to keep going. When the gas tank is empty, we don't fill it with nonsense like apple juice, soda, or olive oil. If we put those in it, instead of helping, we will damage the car. We know the only thing that can make our cars work is fuel or the power source designed for that particular vehicle to operate on. In short, we know there is only one answer to an empty gas tank. Why do we think our spiritual lives are any different?

When it comes to our spiritual lives, we seem to be confused about what should be filling our emptiness. Some of us fill it with derogatory music, some with people, some with alcohol or other medication, and still, some with sex and social media. It takes us forever to realize that we are filling ourselves up with meaningless things that can be destructive. It appears that only in the midst of the damage we ask ourselves, "When was the last time I listened to some worship and praise music? When was the last time I cracked open my Bible and meditated on God's Word? When was the last time I called on the name of Jesus?"

Let's take a story from the first book of the Bible to illustrate what happens when we give something outside of God the opportunity to fill us.

The Bible reference is Genesis 3:1-7. This is the story of Eve and when she ate the fruit from the forbidden tree. The same tricks the serpent used that day on Eve are the very ones the Devil uses today. So, pay attention and learn how you can prepare against the Devil's schemes. He only has power over you if you give it to him. Why did Eve look to something created to fill her up as opposed to looking to her Creator? Why do we do the same? One reason is because we invite conversation. Eve entertained the conversation with the serpent. Eve entertained the conversation with the serpent.

The serpent came up to Adam and Eve and asked "Did God really say?"

Sometimes, we indulge in shows and movies that pose the same question. We watch these scenes and reason with ourselves saying, "Well, it's not that bad; they aren't actually doing anything, and it's just a movie." Instead of skipping the scene or exiting from the movie altogether, we continue to watch and be persuaded by our desires. Remember that the serpent asked them, "Did God really say?" It's all about a loophole. We think that because the film is open to the public and there are no restrictions due to graphics that there is a sense of innocence we can hold on to. "It's just a kiss." You're right. You are absolutely right. It is just a kiss until a kiss becomes common and boring and you want something more.

Fun facts: The first on-screen kiss was in 1896[1], and the first on-screen open mouth kiss was in 1926[2]. The first sex scene was in 1933[3], and by 1968, different levels of nudity became permissible for on-

---

[1] Popova, Maria. "The First Kiss in Cinema, 1896." *The Atlantic*, Atlantic Media Company, 24 Jan. 2012, www.theatlantic.com/entertainment/archive/2012/01/the-first-kiss-in-cinema-1896/251812/#:~:text=It%20comes%20as%20no%20surprise,frowned%20upon%20by%20Victorian%20society.

[2] Scott, A. O. "A Brief History of Kissing in Movies." *The New York Times*, The New York Times, 10 Dec. 2014, www.nytimes.com/2014/12/14/magazine/a-brief-history-of-kissing-in-movies.html.

[3] Sheep, et al. "The First Onscreen Orgasm in the History of Cinema and the Actress Who Performed It - Art-Sheep." *Art*, 24 Aug. 2016, art-sheep.com/the-first-onscreen-orgasm-in-the-history-of-the-cinema-and-the-actress-who-performed-it/.

screen films[4] with a few restrictions. My point is we went from "It's just a kiss" to "Here is a whole human, unashamed for all to see and be captivated by." So "Did God really say?"

We run the risk of giving other things access to fill us up when we entertain the conversations that tickle our curiosity outside of God's protection. A relationship with God comes with commands that are put in place not to limit our existence but to protect our lives from things seen and unseen that could if left unchecked draw us farther away from God's promises. Impatience and doubt for example, can cause us to entertain a plethora of conversations when we grow tired of waiting on the promises of God.

Eve turned from being flat-footed in God's word to doubting whether she understood His word in the first place. "You will not certainly die." It is so easy to be fooled by words, when we don't trust the One who spoke them. The minute we lose trust in God is the very moment the Enemy comes strolling in so he can plant seeds of doubt in what we once knew to be the truth. That doubt then gives our flesh an excuse to scratch our curiosity. Whoever said doubt always had to feel bad? We have this funny habit of blaming our sin decisions on the devil, except that the devil has no power over you as a believer. He can't make you eat the cake. He can bake it in front you, cover it with frosting, set the table, and even prepare a seat for you, but the devil cannot make you sit and eat. Sometimes doubt is an excuse to do what we think feels right, for example, having a slice of cake. I'm not talking about the same kind of cake if you get my drift. Instead of being specific I'd rather you relate it to whatever a slice of cake looks like for your specific situation. But cake is not of the Devil. However, cake outside of the proper time and out of order can ruin a meal. You could be

---

[4] "Motion Picture Association Film Rating System." *Wikipedia*, Wikimedia Foundation, 11 July 2020, en.wikipedia.org/wiki/Motion_Picture_Association_film_rating_system.

thinking, "But it's so sweet and it feels right." Yeah, maybe – at first until it starts to eat away at you physically, emotionally, and spiritually. It feels right until you no longer feel right in your own skin.

In the same way, the fruit in Eve's hand looked good and was pleasing to the eye. Hint, hint, temptation doesn't look like a toothless rat staring across at you on the kitchen counter. It looks like your favorite meal, you know the one that makes your mouth start to water before its even on your plate. The fruit in Eve's hand was not bad. After all, it was in the garden of Eden. What resulted in eating the fruit outside of God's permission was bad. When Adam and Eve ate the fruit of the tree of knowledge of good and evil, their eyes were opened. They saw their nakedness and in utter shame ran and hid from their Creator—the same Creator who called them good when He made them.

We could argue that shame was something God never wanted us to feel. Shame are the chains that make it difficult to believe we are royalty. Shame silences our tongues from responding to the call. Shame will have us die in silence while screaming from the inside that we want to be set free. Shame is the fruit of self-doubt that we let sit on the inside of us. Shame is of the Devil. The fruit is not. By passing on the meal to eat the cake just because the meal is not yet ready to eat doesn't then qualify the cake as the thing to satisfy our hunger. Sure, we may eat the cake and feel full, but as our body breaks it down, the sugar will convert into short term energy and the aftermath of a sugar high doesn't make it worth it. Instead, after consuming a number of useless calories, we end up feeling empty and even hungrier. This time around instead of reaching for another slice of cake, let's wait patiently for the meal. Everything has a time and a place. But again, this is our salvation – that every slice of cake we've already eaten to this point and will eat in our weakness in the future will not be held against us when we repent. But do not use this as an excuse to take advantage of God's grace.

To return to what I said before, when we doubt what we know, we doubt the one who told us what we know.

Eve became a victim to the Devil's warped interpretation of God's word. She ate the forbidden fruit and in doing so, she also doubted God. Why do we doubt the instructions of the gardener while eating the fruit he planted? If I am walking down a trail and I go to grab what looks good to my eyes and completely ignore any warning signs about the safety of eating whatever I find, I would certainly be a fool to eat it anyway. Perhaps the person who put up the warning sign had a reason to do so in the first place. Similarly, Eve was aware of the warning and yet her desire to satisfy her curiosity got the best of her. Eve's first mistake, however, was not to bite into the yummy fruit. Her first mistake was to get in proximity to what she had been warned to stay away from. Why enter the bakery and pretend that the smell of the freshly baked goods isn't going to convince you to pull out your money? I am Eve, Eve is me. I've made this same mistake more times than I can count, and it wasn't until I removed myself from the situation that I was able to flee temptation.

Sometimes I foolishly convince myself that I am in total control. Maybe you can relate? I imagine this is how Adam and Eve felt as they creeped closer and closer toward the forbidden fruit. They were probably thinking to themselves, "We got this. We're just going to take a look and then we will slowly back away. No harm, no fowl." However, by placing themselves in proximity to the forbidden fruit, Adam and Eve also made themselves vulnerable to the devil's trap.

So, here is the thing. If you are looking for the devil, you can always find Him in the places you aren't supposed to be or in the conversations that aren't supposed to take place. The devil cannot be everywhere at once. Unlike God, the devil is not omnipresent. He is, however, strategic. If you can't be everywhere at once, but you want to catch someone in a trap, what better place to catch them then

26

somewhere they aren't supposed to be, maybe somewhere in a dark corner?

So how did Adam and Eve get caught in the devil's trap? Well, after having put themselves in a place of vulnerability, they entertained a conversation. "You will not certainly die." Those were the devil's words. He didn't even have to convince them, he just had to get them to doubt what they heard while he had them right where he wanted them. How do we know for sure that Adam and Eve doubted God's warning about the forbidden fruit? It is because they went to check it out for themselves. Hmm? Sound familiar?

Adam and Eve did half of the work by coming into proximity of what was off limits for their own protection. While it is pointless to replay the past, history can be a very helpful tool for the future. Knowing that proximity is just as dangerous as entertaining a conversation, I'd rather now take the long way around just to be safe.

Falling into these entrapments causes us to miss out on the blessings that were already in our grasp. We miss out on blessings that our hands now have no room to receive because they are busy holding the forbidden fruit we are tempted by. In Genesis 3:22b God said, "He must not be allowed to reach out his hand and take also from the tree of life and eat, and live forever." Plainly this means that we can't do life our way and have access to God's promises. A lukewarm existence is not what God wants for us. We cannot be covered in sin and live forever or else we will surely die. Adam and Eve forfeited a blessing they had access to (the tree of life) for a disability. They laid down their crowns to pick up a walking stick.

What happens next? When we read verse 23 and onward, we learn that God didn't remove the blessing. Instead, He removed Adam and Eve's access to the blessing. Adam and Eve went from living a lavish life to working the ground. Don't get me wrong. They lost access to a blessing, but God didn't stop blessing them. The earth produced fruit for them to eat and live, and they also bore children.

They could have been walking around in the garden of Eden eating the fruit of the earth, which God had already planted but because of their disobedience, they had to plant the seed, wait for it to grow, then eat.

Another story in the Bible we can turn to is that of Abraham and Sarah. God gave them a promise (Genesis 15:4-5). They heard it and understood, but then they entertained a conversation, created space to doubt their understanding of what they heard, and by association, doubted the Creator. They entertained doubt and that doubt enticed them to devise a plan to produce children out of their strength - completely circumventing God's plan for them. This resulted in Ishmael (Genesis 16:1-5). The promise was Isaac and they got him anyway, but it came at a price for Hagar and her son, Ishmael. The rest of the story is found in Genesis Chapters 15 and 16. In the same way, when we allow the world to fill us, we (or the people around us) experience struggles we were never meant to: depression, anxiety, loneliness. Hence, we miss out on our blessings because we get involved in something we have no business dipping our toes into.

Is it ever worth it?

Eve didn't become like God. She was already like God because she and Adam were made in His image. When God looked at them, just as He did all He had created, He saw it was good (Genesis 1:31). Yet, just one bite later, not only were Adam and Eve in a rush to hide from each other, they also made an effort to hide from God. What does it mean to be created in God's image? More importantly, why do we hide ourselves from God? We have characteristics that are evident in our Father such as a will, dominion and through Christ we are righteous, we have power, and light just to name a few. The difference is God has all authority and dominion.

We do not look like God in terms of facial resemblance. But just as Jesus explains in John 14, because we know Him, we know the Father and because we've seen Him, we've have seen the Father. In the same way, we are created in God's image so that when others see us, when they meet us, speak with us, have an exchange with us - they see Jesus. We hide from God because our sin makes us feel unrecognizable. This is the same reason why many of us don't bother checking ourselves out in the mirror after Thanksgiving and Christmas. It is because we do not expect to find the same dimensions that were there before we had overindulged. Disobedience makes us feel unrecognizable.

When Eve made a decision outside of the unity that existed between her and God, she didn't gain what she was expecting. Instead, her decision to experience the potential for more opened her eyes (Genesis 3:6-7). Let me explain. I believe when the Word said "knowing good and evil," it wasn't referring to a "read in a book" grasp of good and evil. I think it is referencing the tangible and attached experience of good and evil. For example, you can read and do research on Jamaica as an amazing vacation destination, but until you experience it for yourself, you won't really know.

In Genesis Chapter 2 when God woke Adam up from his nap, Adam looked at Eve and was struck by what he saw. He spat out poetry saying "This is now bone of bone, flesh of my flesh." Genesis 2:25 says, "Adam and his wife were both naked, and they felt no shame."

Shame builds a wall that makes it difficult for us to imagine a relationship with God because of how unclean we are in comparison. Our poor decisions in tangent with our sinful nature create feelings of shame. By default, shame can lead to the death of our confidence and convictions about who God says we are. Not feeling sure of who we are can feel like emptiness. I know from personal experience how my relationship decisions weighed heavily on whether I believed God called me or not and if I could still do everything, He asked me to do.

Most importantly, shame will throw us into the battle of our minds. We will try desperately to overcome our past while reconciling our present for the future. I read a quote that is a perfect reminder for this predicament, "If you think you've blown God's plans for your life, rest in this: You, my beautiful friend, are not that powerful" (Lisa Bevere). Despite our many mistakes, God's love for us is all-encompassing. He sacrificed His one and only Son Jesus, so the shame, sins, and mistakes we make daily would not stop us from having a relationship with Him.

Thank You, Jesus, for Your sacrifice because without it, we'd be all alone and empty.

Are you wondering why God seems distant or if He is punishing you? When God kicked Adam and Eve out of the garden of Eden, He didn't do so because He was disappointed (even though He was). God removed them from the garden to redeem them from their sinful nature and its consequences. To come back to Him holy and blameless, sin had to die first, and they had to be born again. Sin could not be allowed to live forever. Hence, Jesus came to conquer sin, death, and the grave. His blood redeemed us and when He died, He broke sin's stronghold over our lives, so we might live and put away the things that cannot satiate our hunger. His blood fills those who choose to accept Him as their Lord and Savior, and He covers all of their blemishes. He is the Living Water and in Him, we shall not thirst or hunger for anything. In Christ, we have eternal life with God.

When We Eat with Christ Jesus

Are you hungry? This is your reminder to stop filling yourself with things that are meaningless, temporary, and incapable of fueling you. By the way, it isn't your stomach that is yelling for food but your soul. In John 6:35, Jesus declares, "I am the bread of life. Whoever comes to me will never go hungry, and whoever believes in me will never be thirsty." In John 14:6, again Jesus tells us, "I am the way and the truth and the life. No one comes to the Father except through me." In Revelation 3:30, Jesus says, "Here I am! I stand at the door and knock. If anyone hears my voice and opens the door, I will come in and eat with that person, and they with me." Don't let your soul go hungry. In John Chapter 15, God tells us to remain in Him, and He will remain in us. Family, let's get it together. There's only one table I'm trying to eat at, and it is in heaven. Every other table is a distraction and will leave us hungrier than we started.

Let's talk about what happens when we stay focused on the promises of God and bypass the treats on the way to His table. I think a great story to explain this is Joseph's story. I really like Joseph's story because his life is a model of what it looks like to obey and persevere knowing that the prize, in the end, is worth it.

In Genesis Chapter 39, Potiphar's wife tempts Joseph to sleep with her, but he refuses to engage in the act. In her embarrassment, she accuses him of attempted sexual assault. Unwilling to hear Joseph's side of the story, Potiphar throws him into prison. Joseph spent years in that prison for something he did not do; yet, he remained faithful. Despite his circumstance, God was with him and blessed everything he did. Joseph always found favor in the eyes of those around him. In Genesis Chapter 41, we find that years later, his name and ability to interpret dreams were brought to the attention of the Pharaoh after he had a dream he did not understand. When he asked Joseph to interpret the dream, Joseph said, "I cannot do it...but God will give Pharaoh the answer he desires." Let us pause right there for a second. We know that Joseph was falsely accused, and we also know that despite his innocence he was thrown into prison and stuck there for years. Despite how unfair life was, he never once forgot the Lord his God and His hand on his life. Even in the presence of Pharaoh, Joseph refused to take credit for something he could not do. He had a talent and he was going to use it to bring a return on God's investment. Can God trust you with what He gave you despite your circumstance?

Joseph, through the Spirit of God, interprets Pharaoh's dreams and then goes one step further by giving him a suggestion. Joseph could have stopped at interpreting the dream. However, he was not doing this for Pharaoh but for God's glory. Using his gift of wisdom, he devised a plan to help Pharaoh save his people. Seeing that the advice was good, Pharaoh said, "Can we find anyone like this man, one in whom is the spirit of God?"

Hallelujah!

Joseph went from having big dreams in the safety of his home to being sold into slavery in a foreign country to serving a respected man in the Pharaoh's army, and then to prison, just to get to this point where Pharaoh could say to him, "Since God has made all this known to you, there is no one so discerning and wise as you. You shall be in charge of my palace, and all my people are to submit to your orders. Only with respect to the throne will I be greater than you...I hereby put you in charge of the whole land of Egypt" (Genesis 40:39-41).

Wow. This is what happens when we choose to be filled by God. When God is with us, we bypass the treats to sit and eat at the table. This is what happens when we feed our souls and not our curiosity. This is what happens when we obey. Life is not fair but neither is favor. Let favor open doors for you that your hands, no matter how strong or wide, could never open. There is access and overwhelming, overflowing favor in the Lord.

Here is the most amazing part of the story. Joseph never had dreams of becoming second in command to Pharaoh. However, his dreams and vision did come to pass just as God had shown him when he was a younger man. I say all this to remind you of what Ephesians 3:20 tells us about God: "He is able to do exceedingly and abundantly, above all you can ask or think, according to the power that works in us." Let us do as Joseph did, and as Ephesians 3:21 says —to God be all the glory.

I don't know about you but I have two things to say:

1. I'm full
2. In the words sung by Detrick Haddon, "God is able to do just what He said He would do. He's going to fulfill every promise to you. Don't give up on God because He won't give up on you. He's able!"

It may feel as if God hasn't kept His promise to you and maybe that's why you walked away, but God has not forgotten you. The fact that you are still breathing is evidence of that. This breath in our lungs can leave as easily as it comes. Let God fill your hungry places and trust that when you receive what He has for you, you won't have enough space to handle it. Your stomach won't be the only thing screaming about how full you are.

My message here is to encourage you to live your life for the LORD your God, and you will never regret it. Give it all to God, not just the drugs and alcohol, friends who don't bring you closer to God, or your job and family but also your life. Choose to be a living sacrifice (emphasis on *living* because to truly live is to be in Christ who is life). To be a sacrifice is to surrender your will, choices, and options to God. Obedience has so many blessings. You can go through a lot of struggles because of the betrayal of friends or the anointing on your life. One lifestyle will leave you full and the other empty.

Let's pray. Dear Lord, I thank You for this Word. I pray that those who can identify with feeling hungry or empty will open themselves to You and shut off all other distractions. May they give You the opportunity to fill them up. Fill us up, Lord, until we overflow. I pray in Jesus' name. Amen.

CHAPTER 3:

IT ENDS WITH ME

"I surrender all to you, everything I give to you
Withholding nothing, withholding nothing
Withholding nothing, withholding nothing"
— *William McDowell*

Dear God,
   It ends with me.

....

Isaiah 64:8 reads, "Yet you, Lord, are our Father. We are the clay, you are the potter; we are all the work of your hand." God says, in Jeremiah 18:6, "Like clay in the hand of the potter, so are you in my hand, Israel."

My favorite moments are when I sit back, reflect, and wonder about all God has brought me through. I am between laughter and tears as I consider the journey even now. Every time, I reflect on my journey and compare it to where I stand today, I try to remember the moment it happened. The moment every burden, ever mistake, and every ounce of shame was removed from my shoulders.

These were the moments He made me strong despite my weaknesses and vulnerabilities. In these moments, I am overwhelmed with gratitude. Gratitude owed to my Father in heaven who infiltrated my broken heart. It is in these moments that I say, "Thank You, Jesus, because You who are clean and holy came into my mess with arms stretched wide. Thank You, Jesus because who I was yesterday didn't come with me into today."

Admittedly, it is far easier to look back at what God has brought me through than to live in and experience being stretched, broken, and remolded. In the following chapter, I will refer to an encounter with Jesus as a bridge we have to cross. Arriving at the bridge is something that many believers, in fact, every believer who has encountered Christ personally comes face-to-face with at multiple points in their lives.

The bridge does not look the same for everyone because none of our journeys are the same. However, many of us face similar bridges but in different seasons. For example, in any given season the Holy Spirit also known as the Spirit of truth (John 16:13) may counsel me to work on self-control or the spirit of offense. While I am working on self-control and out of the spirit of offense, the Holy Spirit could have you working on forgiveness and patience.

True story, forgiveness is something I had to learn. There was a season in my life when one big offense and then a bunch of little offenses would take place at the same time. It felt like getting pricked by a needle every time I came in contact with someone. My heart hardened with each betrayal and offense. I couldn't let go of the hurt. To be honest, I didn't want to let go of it because my hardened heart had transformed into my armor. While my heart was my armor, my memory of the event became my protective lenses with UV light protection at no extra charge. I would be so hurt that I refused to see any light the individual possessed.

This may sound crazy to those who forgive easily. But forgiveness did not come easy for me. Understand that I have introverted characteristics. In speaking for myself alone, not only was I picky about whom I opened myself to, but I was also quick to cut off anyone in that small circle who dared to hurt me. Yes, I said dared to hurt me. That was how far away I was in reflecting God's grace, mercy, and forgiveness to others in my life. You hurt me and I would be done with you. I had no time or energy for repeated hurt or drama. I would rather stay home in my bed watching TV or reading a book than to be out with people and taking the risk of trusting them with my heart and space.

But then I came to a bridge not too long after having crossed a previous bridge. At the previous bridge, God taught me to rely on Him and to communicate with His Spirit in everything. He drew me to that bridge after breaking me—gracefully. He went from teaching me how to be in communion with Him to putting me face-to-face with people. He kept asking me to speak to people and to love them as He loves me. He urged me to bless them even as they spoke behind my back, misused, mistreated, or took advantage of me. He made me face my hardened heart. I'm not perfect now; believe me, but I have no doubt about my progress. Thus, I share my experiences with you in hopes that it will help you break free.

So here it is. After God had changed my heart toward people and made it more like His (quicker to forgive and more willing to welcome than to shut out), He reminded me of where I was just a year before. Just a year before God showed me how I had held on to the pain caused by someone who was supposed to encourage and mentor me. Not only had I hardened my heart against the person, but I had also hardened my heart against the people and things connected to them. He showed me how it took me over a year to forgive them and move past the offense. In other words, healing was necessary. I was walking around angry for over a year and was very bitter about how things played out in my life. I was heavy for over a year and didn't know it until God changed my heart and lifted the burden I had refused to let go. I thought I was strong to protect my heart and my space but instead, I ended up carrying a burden that was stunting my growth. It didn't matter how tall my heels were, my spirit could not stretch beyond where I'd capped the roof of my love.

With every new bridge comes a new challenge. God sees us as His children and like any good and faithful parent, He wants us to grow up and grow up strong.

Don't get me wrong; in the beginning, every time I came face-to-face with a new area God wanted to change in me, all I could see was the drop from the bridge. He would ask me to put my vulnerability on the line and trust Him. Suffice it to say, it was difficult. At first, all I saw were the risks. The risk of losing friends, facing fears, the risk of growing pains, exposure, mistakes, and ridicule. But I practiced trusting

God with my vulnerabilities and learned to fix my eyes above—confident that what I saw in Jesus Christ could never be compared to the drop below (Hebrews 12:1-3). My vulnerabilities and weaknesses—our vulnerabilities and weaknesses—are safe with our Father. It is when we cross the bridge that we find an overflow of God's peace pouring into us exceedingly and abundantly above all we can think or imagine (Ephesians 3:20-21).

It is crucial that we cross these bridges ourselves so our children and our children's children for generations to come can be free of unforgiveness, greed, lack of self-control, anger, bitterness, and so much more. Let these undesirable things end with us.

Moving Forward

When we look to Matthew 14:22, we find a story of what "could have been" but wasn't. It is the story of when Peter took his eyes off of Jesus and was overwhelmed by his surroundings. He saw what he wanted, which was to be where Jesus was, walking on water (Matthew 14:28), but then the wind blew. Unfortunately, in that split moment, Peter went from offering Jesus his vulnerability to rescinding that offer and succumbing to what looked like impending danger. Peter walked on water for a moment and then began to sink. Isn't it funny how we like to believe God with full faith when the promise looks feasible but the minute the winds blow and waves bounce against our ankles, we're ready to back down? Is crazy faith only for "possible promises" and "crazy" where faith is actually required? In verse 31, Jesus says, not just to Peter but also to us, "You of little faith...why did you doubt?"

Decide today that doubting God is a thing of the past. We must learn to fix our eyes on Christ and not on the wind blowing to our left and right. Peter could have reached Jesus, if he had not doubted that he could get through the storm. What is the storm? The storm is part of the process. The storm is meant to build you and make you more adept at maneuvering the wind and the waves. The storm is inevitable, and it doesn't change the fact that the destination is guaranteed. Imagine how far we could have made it if we trusted Jesus through the process. Imagine how far we will go when we hand over the process to Him and press towards our destination.

I want to make it to my promise, so delay ends with me. Will delay end with you too? Will you trust God through the process? I have no choice but too, after all, I can't do life without Him. No more regrets. Here on out, every ounce of sweat, every tear, every scratch that draws blood is a seed going towards the blessed generational legacy that comes out of me. I ain't a slave anymore. I'm free and my children will be free too. There's no time to look back. I like salt but only in my food. I'm looking before me and I'm choosing to move forward. Why? Because it has to end with me!

CHAPTER 4:

FOLLOWING THROUGH

Dear God,

I have so many ideas that I really believe are inspired by You. If any of those visions have not borne fruit because of my laziness or incomplete faith, please give me the strength to press and take action. Help me so that I can wake up a little earlier and stay up a little later. May I be convicted by Your Holy Spirit to get my work done.

I know You've called me for more. I don't want to leave here until I've done everything You've assigned to me. Please forgive me for every moment I've taken advantage of the time. I want to make good use of all You give me and live for Your glory.

....

There is this huge part of me that knows I can do more in a day. Every morning, I wake up with a new idea, new hope, new vision, and dreams I hope to one day be able to look back at and celebrate. But most nights, I prepare for bed the same way I've always done—as though nothing has changed—no new ideas, no new hopes, or revelations. Before I know it, my mornings and nights have become one. The different seasons are the only reason I recognize the time has changed. Have you experienced this feeling of time walking right past you? This is usually a time when we look up and say, "Hey, we have something to celebrate today" like Thanksgiving, Christmas, and the first major snowstorm. This is also about the time we all look up from the treadmill that is our lives (moving but never arriving) and remember we had things we said we wanted to do but never started. This feeling of losing time does one of two things to a person. We either kick it into overdrive or we go back to business as usual.

Too many of us are stuck in the routines of the latter response because we've become complacent to the thought without the action. We do the little things to feel as if we've accomplished it all. But the little things don't mean much in the grand scheme. We keep ourselves busy, always moving but never arriving. We've changed our lives and though our network of impact has grown, we haven't left anything behind that says, "I was here. This is my legacy!"

I don't want to wake up one day thinking, "I should have" or "I could have" or "I wish." As I sit and execute this vision, I realize that this fear of wasting time does not have to be my reality. I say this just as confidently knowing that my introverted nature was never meant to hold me back but propel me forward. I've never wished upon a star and there's no power to be found in it. Instead, I put my hope in the One who executed His vision and placed every star where He wanted it to shine from the very beginning of creation. The crazy part about it is that that same God lives in me and you. The amazing part about that is if you still have breath, it's not too late. My hope is that this chapter motivates you to get out of the rut you are in, to start building, and to follow through to the end. You are here too, and you can leave behind a legacy like a roadmap for others to follow.

We need to learn to follow through with the things we set our hope on. To start, we must get off our treadmills. The treadmill is the symbol of our routines. We get on it and we're moving and sweating but when we get off, we end up right back where we started. This idea brings to mind a well-known verse that I have seen believers use in a similar way—all talk and no follow-through. Please allow me to draw your attention to Habakkuk 2:2: "Write it down and make it plain." It is a really powerful verse because of its simplicity. The concept is to write something down so the vision is clear. Following this routine both motivates and encourages you. It can make us feel we've already accomplished so much. It's similar to how focused we feel when we've created our to-do list for the week or our grocery list for the month. Too often, we put our hope solely in manifesting something by speaking it or writing it down. Too often, we forget that our actions carry just as much if not more weight. Have you created a grocery list? Great! But what we write down on paper won't fill our refrigerators without the follow-through. Until we take the necessary steps to go to the grocery store to buy what we wrote down, day after day, we will walk away from the refrigerator disappointed because it is still empty.

This disappointment at unaccomplished plans reminds me of the words found in Proverbs 13:12: "Hope deferred makes the heart sick, but a longing fulfilled is the tree of life." I want each of us to have a healthy heart instead of a disappointed one. Let's take the first step in healing our hearts and following through so we can live the life God planned for us in the beginning. Transformation is personal and can't take place without you.

First, let's understand the context of Habakkuk 2:2. Then let's talk about executing the vision. Once we've done this, we can have an honest conversation about how the refusal to transform our minds suffocates our hope, visions, and dreams.

Write It Down & Make It Plain

Before we can understand the power in following through with what we write down, I think it is important to understand where and how this popular phrase was originally used. As we learned in grade school, to understand the word or the sentence we're reading we have to look at the context that came before it. We must understand the setup. In the same way, to read Habakkuk 2:2 for understanding, we need to reflect on the previous chapter.

When we read the first chapter of Habakkuk, we find ourselves in the middle of a conversation between Habakkuk, a prophet, and God. Habakkuk asks God to intervene on the injustice taking place around him amongst God's people (Habakkuk 1:3). God explains in so many words that He has something cooking in the kitchen that Habakkuk couldn't imagine. He proceeds to share with the prophet His plans to utilize Babylon (a greedy nation that glorifies itself) to discipline His people Israel (Habakkuk 1:5-6).

In response to this revelation, Habakkuk immediately changes his plea. He goes from complaining to God about the mess of his fellow brethren to defending them. In verse 12 and 13 Habakkuk says:

> *Lord, are you not from everlasting? My God, my Holy One, you will never die. You, Lord, have appointed them to execute judgement; you, my Rock, have ordained them to punish. Your eyes are too pure to look on evil; you cannot tolerate wrongdoing. Why then do you tolerate the treacherous? Why are you silent while the wicked swallow up those more righteous than themselves?*

So, what happened here? Why did Habakkuk change his mind about his brethren being disciplined? It is because he didn't want God to use a nation he felt was beneath him and his brethren to discipline them for their sins. I guess Habakkuk already had an idea about what he wanted God to do and this was not it.

Has this ever happened to you? You beg God to change your situation, to come down and make a way. When He does, you say, "Nah God, I didn't mean for you to do it that way." How can we think the Bible, the Old Testament is no longer relevant in our lives today? We respond as Habakkuk did when we ask God for something, and He doesn't do it the way we pictured. Then we try to stop Him in His tracks.

God responds to Habakkuk in the second chapter, instructing him to:

> *Write down the revelation and make it plain on tablets so that a herald may run with it. For the revelation awaits an appointed time; it speaks of the end and will not prove false. Though it lingers, wait for it; it will certainly come and will not delay.*

First, God instructs Habakkuk to write down the revelation concerning the Babylonians and the Israelites. I write things down so I don't forget and to keep me accountable for my words and actions. But God asked Habakkuk to write it down, as evidence of His judgment. Therefore, when it came to pass, the Israelites would know it was not a coincidence but His directive. God also said to make the revelation plain. It is easy to have an idea but if it is not clear, we won't be able to execute it. So, it is important to break things down into smaller parts so that they are clear and feasible.

Let's consider this cooking example. Let's assume this is my first time preparing a Thanksgiving feast for my family. Creating a reminder on my phone with a note that says "Making Thanksgiving dinner this year" is not enough. I must break it down into categories I can handle. I should know who's coming, what I am making, what ingredients I will need, what allergies I must be aware of, when I am buying the ingredients, how early I will need to start prepping and cooking, what time I should set my alarm for, and more. For some, simply saying "Thanksgiving at my house this year" is enough to get the ball rolling, but for people like me, I need to go a step further. I must strategize how I want to tackle Thanksgiving dinner. I need to know the action steps so I can follow through. Setting reminders and saving ideas on my phone help me do that.

There is another element to what God was instructing Habakkuk to have with this revelation: faith. Whether you are a believer or non-believer, you exercise your faith when you say and act upon what you hope to achieve. For example, if you say you want to graduate from high school with honors or buy a car, you must take action to study hard or save a portion of your paychecks.

As believers, we can trust God to do what He says. Moreover, He communicates His promises differently to various people. He asked Habakkuk to write down the promise. However, He may ask others to share it with a close friend or a stranger. On the other hand, He may ask that we wait patiently and watch as His promise unfolds. No matter how God communicates His promises to us, when we move on His Word and see it come to pass, we will certainly recognize that the glory belongs to Him alone.

For example, God told me I would be hired at my first job out of college. Well, technically, He showed me in a dream. Let me start from the beginning. I was hired as a temporary worker for my first job out of college. For anyone unfamiliar with this, it means that I was hired through a temp agency. This means that though I interviewed with the company and worked for them, I was not their direct employee.

Some downfalls of working for an agency is that you are required to do the same amount and type of work as everyone else who was hired regularly, but for less pay, no benefits, no sick time off, no holiday pay—you get my point. After months of working as a temporary worker, I learned a few things about my office. First, more than half the people I worked with for hours on end were also temporary workers. Some of them had been there for a handful of years.

This leads me to the second point. I found out that not everyone who is a temporary worker is hired full-time with the company. More often than not, temporary workers end up being fired, (released) or they stay on as temporary workers.

Not to mention, I was the freshman on my team. So when hiring season came back around, the others would likely get first dibs. Hopeful and only slightly worried, I prayed about this situation. I brought my desire to God and was at peace with whatever decision He wanted to make. If I was released from the job, then cool, and if I was going to be hired, it was fine too. I can't recall how much time went by, but it wasn't long after that I had a dream. In that dream, I was walking into the lobby of my office and as I walked by the reception desk, I overheard a conversation taking place in the conference room in front of me. Normally, it's basically impossible to hear anything that is being said behind the see-through walls of the room. But in that dream, I could hear everything. Peering in, curious about what I was seeing and hearing, I spotted my first boss, then my second boss, and then the top boss. They were pointing at me as I half-walked and half-strolled by the room. I heard a voice say, "Ashley, we want her."

Less than a week later, I was called to human resources. Upon sitting down in the office, they told me I was hired. Of course, I was elated. I was excited, but not because I was being hired as a full-time employee. I knew that would happen. I was thrilled because God had chosen to reveal this truth to me ahead of time. He had written down His promise in my heart and made it plain, so I would understand. Letter in hand, my heart rejoiced to say, "Thank You, Jesus! You did this."

God backs up His Word and promises with action; we must do the same. My hope was not deferred because God followed-through in my life. In this instance, it was quick but some promises take a while to develop. I share this story to say there is power when we write down the vision and make it plain. If you want a better relationship with your siblings or to be more consistent at your job, then write down the vision; make it plain so that you can remember it as shown in Habakkuk 2:2, and follow through.

Perhaps, you are in a situation where you believe God has told you something but it has yet to come to pass. It's difficult. Believe me when I say I understand. The dream about the job was probably one of the quickest turnarounds I have ever experienced. But there are things God has revealed to me that have yet to come to fruition. Lack of tangible fruit does not mean God isn't working. All it means is that the dish He's cooking isn't ready to be served. Sometimes God allows us to see and know things way before the appointed time as a warning. It is a chance for us to prepare ourselves to be ready for that dish.

Think of it this way: if we have yet to digest the last thing we ate, why would we try to stuff ourselves with more food? Instead, we should wait for the food to digest and build up a hunger or create space for the next meal coming, so we can enjoy it in all its goodness. Another example of this is the return of Jesus. The day Jesus ascended into heaven, He told His disciples He would return soon, but in the meantime, He would send one greater than Himself to be our Comforter. What does this mean? Well, Jesus hasn't returned yet and He made this promise thousands of years ago. Just because it hasn't happened yet does not mean it won't happen. In fact, Jesus gave us something to rest on, something to prepare until He returns for us.

Firstly, He gave us a mission (Matthew 28:16-20). Secondly, He gave us the Holy Spirit who is God's Spirit and our Advocate, Comforter, and Counselor (John 14:15-21). The Holy Spirit who is God in the Trinity (God the Father, Jesus the Son, and the Holy Spirit) lives in us, sealing us for the day Jesus will return (2 Corinthians 1:22). All in all, we have everything we need to live a life that is pleasing to God and to be ready when He comes (2 Peter 1:3). This is a hope that believers should hold tightly to because Jesus will return.

All that said and done, we must have faith when it comes to the promises, revelations, and dreams God has placed on our hearts. We must have faith and follow-through even with the little things like our weekly to-do lists and monthly grocery hauls. We must go a step further than writing down the vision and making it plain. We have to execute it. Execution takes faith.

What Is Faith?

I mentioned a little earlier how writing down the vision and the follow-through requires faith. But there is a distinction made about faith in the Word that I think is important for us to highlight.

When we read through Hebrews Chapter 11, we find the accounts of God's faith-filled servants. The text defines faith as "confidence in what we hope for and assurance for what we do not see." How many of us can say based on this understanding of faith, that we have it? The verse basically means that you believe what you do not already have or see. Faith is trusting God for what is not tangible. James Chapter 2 says, "In the same way, faith by itself, if it is not accompanied by action is dead."

Whoa. Okay then. To start, I didn't call your faith dead; God did. You're probably thinking to yourself, "What?! I have faith. I believe and trust that God will make a way. Have I been wasting time?" Calm down. Faith is trusting God to make a way out of no way. He will surely do as He has said, but sometimes, we also have a part to play, which is to take action. God is faithful and trustworthy in all areas of our lives, including the ones we notice and forget daily: being able to breathe, waking up with access to breakfast, and freedom of religion. But there is a part of faith where God is hands-off. I like to think that our Father in heaven who provides all of our needs is the same Father who asks us to exercise, so we can grow. God our Father loves to spoil us. I believe that. But He also wants to grow us. Growing sometimes takes action like exercising our gifts.

God gave us talents to be a blessing to others. This requires faith, not just believing God's promise on our lives, but exercising that belief until what He has told us matches what we see. Sometimes faith requires that we believe God's promises and because we believe them, we will execute them. This is living faith. It is acting on what we believe.

Living Faith

Living faith is not about being moved by the dream, vision, or promise. It is not the feeling of conviction. Living faith is our response. God isn't looking for a reaction but a response. When God gave me the dream about being hired for my first job, I didn't slack in my work ethics; instead, I doubled down. I kept my efforts consistent and was willing to sacrifice more of my time and energy while I waited for what God showed me to come to light. There will be times when God's promise requires our stillness. Other times, that promise will be like a lit candle in a dark alleyway. However it comes, it is a signal for us to press forward. Some blessings will fall into our laps, while we must stand and reach out for others.

This does not mean you can't react. Being a sensitive person, I am easily emotionally triggered by God's revelations. Sometimes I can't stop smiling; other times, I get stuck in my head trying to understand how the math is supposed to add up. On other occasions, I'm left in tears because the vision is unexpected. Reactions are okay. But at some point, we have to come down from the high of the revelation. We must get out of our heads and trust even more that God knows what He's doing. We have to wipe our tears, stand, and take action. The Enemy is great at distracting us when we've received revelation or a promise. We get distracted by busy work, people, worries, and other life issues; as a result, we keep our promises sitting on a shelf. I urge you to stay focused. Write down the vision and make it plain as Habakkuk 2:2 stated. Then you can create a plan of action, set up deadlines, and surround yourself with the Word, as well as people who meditate on the Word. These are people who are ready to uplift and keep you accountable.

I learned that a promise, desire, or dream is an invitation to pursue God. May we not only have living faith, but may we also live in the place of faith.

Heartsick

I say yes Lord. A sick heart is not my portion. I prefer to avoid it at all cost. It takes too much strength pretending everything is okay when it's not. "Hope deferred makes the heart sick, but a longing fulfilled is the tree of life" (Proverbs 13:12).

I was talking to God and telling Him how tired I was feeling. I couldn't understand it because I was sleeping more than enough hours per night. He told me something. He referred me to a verse previously mentioned that I knew but didn't apply to my life situation. He told me that hope deferred makes the heart sick. My heart was sick. Then, He gave me a word. He said, "Finish." Wanting to understand what He meant by that, I began to reflect. I tried to pinpoint the moment when my heart became sick. It came to me quickly. It all started the moment I realized I wasn't going to be a lawyer. I believed that I would be a lawyer since I was in fifth grade. So to discover that my biggest dream and hope in the world wasn't going to happen—well, it's easy to see why my heart grew sick.

To make a long story short, God told me I wasn't going to law school. So within a few days, I closed my study books, pulled my applications, and emailed all my professors, mentors, and others to let them know they no longer had to write the recommendation letter. This all happened in the same season when I had quit my first job out of college and started a new one.

How does the job play into it all? You see, the new job was supposed to be temporary. My plan was to work there for a short period, send in my applications, and wait for a response. When I was hired, I shared as much with the employer. It makes me chuckle every time I think back to this moment, especially seeing how in the middle of my hurt and confusion, God was opening doors to replace the ones that remained locked in my hand.

See, weeks before the end of my time at that office, the same employer who knew I had made plans for law school asked me if I would be interested in staying on longer. Confident that I would get into a school and unwilling to commit to anything long term, I said no.

A couple of weeks later, I was back in her office telling her the change in plans about law school. Without a moment's hesitation, she smiled at me and said she had already called in a few friends from another department about a potential position and was waiting to hear back. A week later, I had an informal interview with my soon to be new boss.

I am not sharing this personal story just to paint a picture, but to make a point, and to warn you. It's easy to look back and think, "Who would have known?" But that's incorrect. God knew the whole time that I wasn't going to be a lawyer. He knew that before He formed me in my mother's womb. The only person this was news to was me. So always ahead of me, God prepared a path for me in a space that was very picky about whom they let into their firm.

Going from that point to now has not been easy. Open doors don't guarantee a happy heart. Consider Joseph whom God blessed tremendously. When he came face-to-face with the brothers who betrayed him, he was overwhelmed by pain before he could reconcile his heart with them (Genesis 42-43).

Similarly, I had to sit down with my loss and reevaluate what was important to me. Was I willing to walk away from God for a career I had misunderstood as my identity? No. I already knew by that point that I couldn't do life without God. So I sat in the pain for a little while all the while reflecting on God's goodness, providence, sovereignty, and faithfulness. Despite the self-inflicted pain due to the plans I had made without consulting God, He allowed me to see His goodness through the rain. I was never meant to follow through with my plans. Up until that point, God had exposed me to different types of law. In my stubbornness, I could not see how unsatisfied I was because my mind was set.

Being heartsick isn't the way I want to live my life. That much I know. I don't like it, and I don't want it. I made a decision in this season of my life to go God's way. I would rather have my heart broken while walking according to God's plan than to grow heartsick walking according to my plan. This is because when I move, I do not know the consequences of the steps I take. But when God tells me to move, He's already ten steps ahead of me and nothing catches Him by surprise. Also, it is so much easier to follow-through when God is your strength.

I should add that before I pulled everything for law school, my heart wanted to be in agreement with God even if my head wasn't. I remember I had prayed a very simple prayer. I do not know why that was the prayer on my heart that day, but I meant every word I said.

I asked God to take over my life, lead me, and never let me do anything that doesn't match His plans or comes to waste my time. You see, God was knocking at my door. He was not knocking on the door to the entrance of my house but on the doors of the inner rooms. When I prayed, it was as if I handed Him the key to do what He wanted with it. Without delay, He started His renovations. He began breaking down one wall after another, replacing a door handle or two here and there, changing the windows, and adding lights to what was once submerged in darkness. I had built a room in my house that was never meant to be orchestrated by God. Sure, I could see He had given me the gifts and capacity, but I had constructed something different from His vision.

Imagine a room in the inner chambers of my house. You know how some people decorate their front doors with floor mats that say, "Welcome" or a door sign to a bedroom that reads "Beware." Well, this particular room that I'd previously kept away from God was called "My Career Choice." After giving Him the key to that room, God did exactly what I expected. He took down the sign that said "My Career Choice" and placed in my hand the new sign "God's Carrier." It means I am a vessel carrying the gifts He already made plans for before my career choice came into play.

Perhaps, like me, you have a couple of rooms you've intentionally or unintentionally noted as off-limits to God. Perhaps years have gone by and as they do, the dust builds up in these rooms. Why? Because it hasn't borne any fruit. You are barren because you watered a seed that was not planted in God's garden. Your faith is not lacking, still you're believing for something God never promised. Our words return to us void when they do not echo the words released by God first (Isaiah 55:11).

My warning to you is simple. Submit yourself to God now, rather than later. I say this because it is easier to obey God from the start than to give up something outside His will that you set your heart on. Obedience is not easy. If it was, you would not have to go against your will. Fighting the desires of your heart to be obedient is even more difficult. It leaves a gap that takes time to heal. This is because you placed hope in something you shouldn't. Ask God first; wait for His response and then act.

You may be thinking, "But isn't it God who placed the desire in me for what I want?" That too is a great question but a wrong one. It is wrong because our desires are influenced by the world around us. You would be better off asking yourself this question: is it my heart's desire to chase after things that cannot satisfy or after the only One who can? Sometimes we confuse what the world tells us we should desire: money, position, space, and titles with what God wants us to desire, which is to live for Him and His glory.

Do not be afraid! Remember Matthew 6:33, "Seek first his kingdom and his righteousness, and all these things will be given to you as well." When we understand this, we will know it is impossible to miss out on anything if we put God first."

To bring it back full circle, what does the well-known verse found in Habakkuk 2:2 mean?

> *Write down the revelation and make it plain on tablets so that a herald may run with it. For the revelation awaits an appointed time; it speaks of the end and will not prove false. Though it lingers, wait for it; it will certainly come and will not delay.*

In the simplest way, this verse means we can trust God. He will not disappoint us as humans do. We can literally bet on God because

His Word is like a tree in a forest: when it falls it will be heard[5] - whether or not you heard it at all.

So, let's write down the vision; make it plain; seek God first in the areas we previously didn't take action, and trust Him to follow-through to the end (Habakkuk 2:2).

Living My Best Life – ACT I

This is how you can be practical about finishing in your life. In each of these steps, you must endeavor to seek God.

Step 1: *Start Small.* This is comparable to learning to trust someone new in our lives. There is nothing wrong with starting small. Trust God in the small things and as you go along, you'll find you can trust Him with the big things too. When you start small, you can celebrate quickly. For example, clean out your closet, rearrange your room, try a new cafe, and see if it inspires you to study more.

Step 2: *Make a List.* After the first victory, you'll feel like you can do anything you set your mind to do. It is a great attitude to have. So make a list of things you'd like to start and finish ranging from small to big projects. As you go, check them off.

Step 3: *Change Up Your Daily Routine.* Challenge yourself to read a chapter of a book before you sleep. Set your morning alarm for 30 minutes earlier than usual. Make breakfast or go to sleep 30 minutes earlier. It doesn't matter what changes you make, as long as they are productive. This simply means that now is not the time to start binge-watching your favorite shows way past your bedtime. You have to get out of the rut by not digging yourself deeper into a new one.

---

[5] Jehookah Jarmon, Gorvenstof, Ukraine

Step 4: *Do It All Over Again!* This time around, get a little more adventurous with your list. Before you know it, you'll be hoping for bigger things than you could ever hope to handle on your own. The minute you recognize God's voice, write down the vision and make it plain. Take action in your living faith and know that with time, the revelation will come to pass. Above all, just keep doing what God told you to do until then.

CHAPTER 5:

POSITION AND POWER

Dear God,

I'm afraid they're going to fire me. I think it's time to pack my bags.

....

How many of us have said this and meant it?

I know His name to be Jehovah-Jireh, my provider. Yet, I believed that with one mistake, I could lose something I never provided for myself. When I look at my life, I can't take credit for maintaining anything I have. The breath in my lungs—God provides. The flow of my thoughts—God provides. The home I lay my head in—God provides. What was I afraid of exactly? God is my source. Everything else is a resource.

Life is not fair. People and things come and go. However, despite all the things and people that change around us, God's omnipotence is unchangeable. We will go through big and small bumps on this rollercoaster ride called life; yet, God will never change. When everything is good, we lift our hands and tell God we will never cease to glorify His name. But when things become worse, we are quick to blame Him. Do we blame God because we put too much power in a single moment? Do we blame God because we are convinced that life could never be good again? Or do we blame God because the thing in front of us does not look like the promise He whispered in our ears?

Perhaps we don't blame Him outright. Instead, we believe the lies of the Enemy who tells us our source has changed His mind about us. Isaiah Chapter 55 warns us that God's ways and thoughts are not like ours. Yet, we compare His nature to human nature. If you take anything from what we will discuss in this chapter, let it be this little, simple thing: do not stop trusting God just because your circumstance doesn't look like the promise. At times, it may feel as if God is distant. Things may look as if they are going in the wrong direction but believe and trust that you will always remain connected. Whether you are aware of that or not solely depends on if you stay in position. Everything else is a lie. Yeah, you messed up, but it isn't over until God says it is over.

Purpose in Position

Our titles and accolades do not give us purpose. These things can accentuate purpose. Titles, degrees, and applause cannot birth purpose. You have purpose without the title. Whether you get in position to fulfill your purpose is a whole other conversation.

John the Baptist for example had purpose before his mother was even born. The prophetic words of Isaiah in Isaiah 40:3 refers to John the Baptist as *"A voice of one calling: 'In the wilderness prepare the way for the Lord; make straight in the desert a highway for our God.'"* Amazing isn't it? John the Baptist had a purpose before he got into position. But in faith, he acted in agreement with it.

Another example is Moses who ran away from the luxurious and protected life of an adopted Jew. Having been raised in the household of the very people who enslaved his kind, Moses seemed to have everything going for him. That is until he killed an Egyptian, got called out for it by his fellow Hebrews, and was called to explain his actions. Confused about who he was and where he belonged, Moses ran away from home and from his people. It was forty years after having run away that Moses learned it didn't matter how far he ran, he couldn't run away from his purpose. You know what God did? God called Moses to get back into alignment with his purpose (Genesis 2:11-15). Accepting God's invitation, Moses prepared himself to go back to the seat he left.

What I am trying to explain is that your employment details, the school you attend, and the family you were raised in are planned and allowed circumstances that can play some role in your purpose, but they don't give you purpose. Stop thinking that God is reacting to your situation. Instead, view your situation as an event God watches unfold as he orchestrated for it to unfold. Hundreds of years before the Hebrews become slaves to Egypt, God told Abraham it would happen. He shared this news in the same moment He promised Abraham, who was childless at the time that he would be the father of a nation (Genesis 15:13).

God wants to cultivate something out of you in these spaces. But coming from these spaces doesn't qualify or disqualify you from God's predetermined purpose for your life. You had purpose before you came into these spaces and experienced the things you did. If we dress ourselves in who God says we are, we would not put so much weight on who we think we are. Who we try to be without God will always be a limited version of the full picture. Living out only a portion of our purpose is like a website getting stuck on the loading page. You haven't arrived yet."

That being said, sometimes circumstance and purpose coincide. Simply put, not every preacher is also the pastor of a church, and not every pastor of a church should be leading a church. But sometimes a preacher is also a great pastor of a church.

What can we do to be purposeful regardless of our circumstance? Well, we can grow. If you are lacking patience then exercise that with the people around you and exercise patience with yourself. If you are struggling in self-control devise a plan so that you win more battles than you lose. If you don't know how to properly take care of your skin, your hair, your health – then work on that and rediscover who you are regardless of your circumstance. Growing is never wasted and can be useful in the next season. Whatever your circumstance, I would also encourage you to remain faithful to God's promise and watch as the page turns, and the promise unfolds before your very eyes.

Our purpose isn't like our home Wi-Fi. It doesn't get lost just because we are temporarily disconnected. It makes me think of David who was out in the field when Samuel, the prophet came knocking on his home door. Every one of his brothers was home but David.

Regardless of the fact that David was temporarily away from his home, he was not at risk of forfeiting his purpose. In fact, his purpose had everyone else waiting on his arrival. Who is waiting on you to arrive? David may not have known the day or the hour that his purpose would come knocking, still it was not an excuse to remain stagnant. When he entered the room where Samuel was waiting, the scriptures describe David as one who was "glowing with health and had a fine appearance and handsome features" (1 Samuel 16:10-13). David looked the part by the time his purpose came around. When the time comes, I hope my purpose doesn't catch me slipping.

That being said, sometimes what feels like backtracking can be the journey that connects us to our purpose. Let's take Joseph as our example. Long story short, God showed Joseph visions and dreams of promotion beyond his imagining (Genesis 37:5). Then his brothers sold him into slavery, he was sexually harassed by his slave master's wife, and later imprisoned for something he did not do (Genesis 37-39). Looks like Joseph's life took a turn for the worse. A complete backtrack from how he likely expected his life to go. Yet this process was a part of the journey to be in alignment with his purpose. God was not trying to catch up to or correct what he had originally showed Joseph in his dreams. All these trials was just part of the process.

It was because Joseph continued to grow regardless of his circumstance that his name was the one Pharaoh called for help. You may wonder how Joseph was able to continue growing while in prison with access to nothing. Well, he grew in his spiritual gifts. In prison, Joseph interpreted the dreams of his cellmates and they came to pass exactly as he said they would. The development of this spiritual gift was the key that gave him access to his predetermined purpose. Do we see how obedience even in difficult circumstances work out for our good?

I can't begin to imagine what was going through Joseph's mind when the captain of the guard pulled him out of prison, shaved his beard, and put some clean clothes on him in Genesis 41:14.

Joseph was being summoned to interpret the Pharaoh's dream. What's the difference between interpreting a cellmate's dream and interpreting Pharaoh's dream? Don't focus on what Joseph was called to do but where he was called to do it. Joseph first interprets a dream while in prison. He was obedient in a low place, in a humbling position, and in a dark time. Now he's being called to interpret a dream in a high place. Let me break it down further. God is calling some of you out of your circumstance. You should have noticed it when he shaved your beard, washed your hair, gave you new clothes and something to eat, but you didn't. It's okay. Notice now. Look around you. You're no longer in the prison that you've existed in for years. You've been called out.

Knock, knock.
Who's there?
It's your purpose.

I love it! Matthew 10:18 says, *"On my account you will be brought before governors and kings as witnesses to them and to the Gentiles."* Joseph was summoned to the Pharaoh's chambers to do what he had done perhaps many times before so that he could point all glory back to God. Luke 16:10 says, *"Whoever can be trusted with very little can also be trusted with much."* Joseph remained faithful in a difficult circumstance and he grew, so much so that when he was called out of prison, he was immediately promoted.

Don't worry about whether you're ready or not. Because you are ready. I can say this confidently because Joseph had the keys to the palace he had been groomed for. He probably didn't know he had the keys until he came face to face with the door. What was the door? The door is the problem for which only you carry the solution.

I can't help but consider the solution Joseph offered the Pharaoh. You see the Pharaoh had a predicament, a problem that he had never before faced and thus could not devise a solution to help manage it. What was his problem? The problem was that there was to come seven years of abundance in harvest, followed by seven years of devasting famine. In other words, the land of Egypt was at risk of disappearing off the face of the planet in a period of fourteen years. What a difficult predicament to be in, right?

Yet somehow Joseph was able to come up with a solution. The same Joseph who had never before directed an entire nation. What was that solution? Joseph's solution for the Pharaoh was to save a portion of the harvest from the good years to be distributed during the famine years to follow. Did you catch it?

Again, I can't help but consider the solution Joseph offered to Pharaoh. Joseph's solution intrigues me because it's something that only someone who's had to survive in a low place could come up with. It is the kind of solution that only someone who had to find the light in a dark space could come up with. Joseph's solution sounds like something he learned from his days in prison.

I imagine that a feast load of food was not portioned out for him every single day. Thus, on the days when we received more food than usual, I imagine that he saved a portion of it for the days, when the prison guards forget he even existed. Joseph had the keys to the palace because in prison, he learned the lessons that would qualify him to take position. You may not appreciate the circumstances that you are in right now, but if you would just learn the lessons that are in that hard place, you would come out of it with the keys to your palace. Joseph's purpose was connected to him all along but when he was summoned higher, his purpose and circumstance coincided.

What a great example for us to model our lives after. Joseph's is a story of patience, perseverance, and obedience among other things. The reality, however, is that many of us get tired of waiting, grow sick of having to push, and eventually we silence the voice of the Holy Spirit. I'm not talking about those of us who don't know Christ. I'm talking to my fellow brothers and sisters in the church. Even now, years later like was Moses' situation – your purpose is still connected to you. But if you aren't moving towards it or walking in purpose, it means you've taken one of two ways out. One you waited until your time on earth ran out or you're deliberately living in disobedience. If you're reading this book than it's the latter and not the former of these two options.

Only Two Ways Out

Like I said, if you're reading this book and you're not moving towards or living in purpose then it means you're deliberately living in disobedience. My desire is not to be harsh. I just don't want to go in circles and throw confetti around the room. I grew up with more siblings than I could count on one hand. If you have even one sister or one brother than you'll understand this same passion I have. Being an older sister, I cannot accept that my younger siblings remain stagnant. I want them to go higher, to be even better than myself, to go after everything God has called them to.

In the same way, this is my desire for you. That you go after God and violently take what is yours. I know the fight is long and its hard. Sometimes you feel like you've made no progress at all. My sister, my brother, I know you can go a little further. Push! Living in disobedience isn't how we want to live out our Christian journey. Don't get stuck on the loading page.

Whatever it is that you think is holding you back whether it is fear, shame, low self-esteem, access, age, influence, or if you're just plain confused – stop overthinking. I know it's easier said than done. But seriously, stop thinking so hard. While in prison, Paul gave instructions on how to live as Christians. One of the many things he says is to stop existing in the futility of our thinking (Ephesians 4:17). We get stuck in fear because we overthink. We get stuck in shame because we overthink. We get confused about which direction to turn in because we're overthinking it. Like Paul says, Christian living requires sensitivity to the Holy Spirit not a dependency on what we think feels good (Ephesians 4:19). Relying on what feels or looks good will keep us stagnant spiritually.

Instead, I encourage to stop running, stop hiding, and stop giving yourself excuses. Just go. Press on. Move forward and trust that God will get you to where you need to be. Remain faithful in that place and watch as the promise unfolds. I'm sure it was difficult for Joseph as one attack was followed by another. Still Joseph learned the lessons, he continued to grow, and before he knew it, he held keys to the palace.

....

Dear God,

They can fire me if they want to. Where you lead me, I will go. Please keep me so I don't fall. I thank you Lord that delay is not denial. I still have purpose and I'm violently going after what you've assigned me to do.

CHAPTER 6:

THIS IS YOUR NOTICE

Dear God,

I will worship You with every inhale and exhale and with every bone in my body.

....

If you are reading this, it is not because your alarm woke you up this morning.

I have a question for you. What are you responsible for doing today that you should have done yesterday?

Tick–tick–tick

Tock

Tick–tick–tick

Tock

"We have everything we need to live a life that pleases God. It was all given to us by God's own power, when we learned he had invited us to share in his wonderful goodness" (2 Peter 1:3). This scripture tells us we have everything we need to complete our responsibilities.

As I look around, it feels as if we've lost our sense of urgency and the desire to live our lives to the fullest. I'm talking about accomplishing everything we set our minds to and all God told us to do. Currently, living our lives to the fullest means out of context self-care, laziness, overspending, and gluttony. All of which results in delayed satisfaction due to uncompleted work. The wise author of the book of Proverbs warns us that "Hope deferred makes the heart sick, but a longing fulfilled is a tree of life." For one reason or another, we look at our dreams and think they are too big for us to bring to life but not too big for our neighbors. That spirit of comparison paralyzes us. We look back at history and think making big moves is a thing of the past. We are so busy looking back at what has been done that we perish away in the present. God tells us in Isaiah 43:18-19 to forget the past because He is doing a new thing. Let Him do that new thing through you.

The stories where people die from good old age are not the stories that cause us to sit up straighter in our chairs. Instead, the stories that get our attention are about the young girl who died from a seizure, the people who died in the middle of the day on an airplane that should not have malfunctioned, the kid who was excited to go to school when the driver lost control of the wheel, the person who was walking home from work or dinner and a movie and was hit by a stray bullet. Perhaps for you it was the healthy individual with everything going for him or her who just didn't wake up; this caused your hands to sweat. I could keep going, but I think you get my point. It is not the stories of people who have lived their lives that make us more aware of our own. It is the people who seem to have so much more life in front of them but die. These stories keep us awake at night. These stories lead us to bow our heads, thank God for every new day and say, "I will rejoice and be glad in it."

So again I say, if you are up this morning it is not because your alarm went off. The ringing of your alarm was a notice on your breath, a notice on your heartbeat, a notice on your mind that you were given another chance.

What will you do with it? What is your assignment?

Here's a hint. It is that thing that makes us kind of uncomfortable when we think of the little progress we've made toward finishing it. It is that thing that just won't leave us alone while we try to go about our daily routines. It is that thing we just can't get out of our heads and spirits that makes it difficult for us to sleep in peace. Consider that it may be the Holy Spirit reminding us of our assignments. It's like an alarm that refuses to let you live in the partially comatose state we call deep sleep. Did you know that deep sleep is as close as a living human's body gets to being in a coma? For many of us, this is our favorite stage of sleep, the stage where the world ceases to exist. How many of us are still sleeping?

It is in moments like these that I am reminded of the power of an assignment. It will keep me awake as I sleep at night. Like a pressing thought even fatigue and pain fail to escape. I can recall one late night or really early morning when God woke me up for an assignment. When I first woke up, I thought perhaps I had heard something that scared me. I have never been a super heavy sleeper so trying to relax my body and shut off my senses, I attempted to return to sleep. There it was again. The urgency—it was heavy. I was in danger—but I wasn't. It wasn't me or my body. Clearing my fatigue, I took a moment to understand. There was nothing happening around me. In fact, I only remember silence. Then I knew my assignment was to pray. I didn't have to think twice as I opened my mouth. I knew exactly what to pray for and that I would not be able to return to sleep until I completed that assignment. Someone needed prayer. Your assignment is not for you; it is for the common good. Your assignment is for your siblings, coworkers, the stranger you bumped into on the crosswalk because your eyes were focused on the phone instead of the triggered stop lights, and for the person who nearly backed their car into you. It's not about you; it is about the souls around you.

Considering how impactful the completion of our assignments are, it makes sense that the pressure to complete them makes it difficult to remain senseless and paralyzed. Even an alarm is defined as an anxious awareness of danger. As dramatic as that may sound, I would say that's an accurate description. An alarm lets us know that we're about to miss out on something, that we could be running late, or that someone or something is waiting for us. All factors considered; we have taught ourselves to snooze through life despite the weight our assignments carry for the souls connected to our obedience. We put the deadline on hold and some of us straight up unplug the thing because we don't want to feel rushed or pressured by anyone.

The snooze button—it's a dangerous thing. Let's talk about it.

Override

Somehow, we have figured out a way to not feel so guilty about putting our lives on hold.

What do I mean by this? I mean we have put our visions for a better future on hold. We have goals to lose weight, start the business, write the book, eat better, sleep earlier, and save more. Yet, as soon as we are given another day to execute the vision, we hit snooze. We say things like, "Oh, I'll start meal prepping on Sunday" or "I'll practice saving more and spending less with the next paycheck," and "Oh, well, I guess I can't go to the gym until I find a new workout partner." Maybe this sounds familiar to you. Weeks before thanksgiving is my favorite execution of the snooze button when my friends and I share our New Year's resolutions. Right in the middle of ignoring the notification in our minds to just put that extra plate of food away for another day, we convince ourselves that waiting another 35 days or more to get healthy is the best decision we can make. We are good at running away from work.

Let's connect this to the Word. If we turn to John Chapter 9, we find that Jesus is presented with an opportunity to work. The fourth and fifth verses read, "As long as it is day, we must do the work of him who sent me. Night is coming when no one can work. While I am in the world, I am the light of the world." Here in this example, Jesus is talking to His disciples as He kneels to heal a blind man. He very clearly has an assignment and wants to complete it while He still has time.

I really like this example because it supports how our assignments both immediate and pending are for the common good. Look at Jesus' life work, for example. He became both God and man so that He could ultimately die for us and reconcile us to God again. That was His ultimate assignment. However, in the 33 years of human life here on the earth, Jesus completed everything else that came along His path. He was baptized, healed the sick, fed the hungry, embraced the children, taught His disciples, forgave sinners, and spoke the truth to the Israelites. While He was still in the world, Jesus did everything God asked of Him.

Now, Jesus knew the exact date and time of His deadline and still, He felt the urgency to get it done. We see this when He stayed behind after the Passover Festival to listen and ask the teachers questions at only 12 years old (Luke 2:46). We are each probably thinking to ourselves, "Well, if I didn't feel like I was behind before, now I feel it." Don't look at your life this way. Instead of looking at the number of years that went by without you noticing, look at the time you have right now to change your legacy. Ask yourself what you can do today. Don't let fears, insecurities, and characteristics stop you from pressing toward the mark as Paul says in Philippians 3:14.

Perhaps we can begin to love as Christ loves us, be a sister, friend, teacher, or leader. Maybe we can get a pen and notebook out, write down the vision, and execute it until it is finished. Maybe we can learn to trust God in our current position, excel where we are, and not focus so much on where we could be. Whatever our tasks, we can rest in the truth that we can do all things through Him who gives us strength (Philippians 4:13). Let us seek our callings and purpose. Let us do everything we can to accomplish as many things on that checklist before the clock runs out. Do not give up before you have even started because every decision could change your legacy.

We may not know our deadlines, but we understand tomorrow is not promised. So let us apply our knowledge, glean wisdom from God's Word, and live lives that are pleasing to Him. Does this mean we will execute everything perfectly or we'll never want to just stand still? Absolutely not! Even Jesus at one point wanted to hit the snooze button. But His mother Mary made sure His feelings didn't delay His assignment.

For example, if we turn our Bibles to John Chapter 2, we will find Jesus at a wedding with His mother. There, the worst possible thing that can happen at such a festivity happened. They ran out of wine. Turning to Jesus, Mary tells Him to convert the barrel of water into wine. Jesus responds, "Woman, why do you involve me? My hour has not yet come." Hold up. Wait a minute. Just like that, Jesus goes to hit the snooze button. But like my mother does when I want to pass on an assignment, Mary ignores His response and proceeds as though Jesus said yes. Just like that, Mary challenges her son to complete the task she set for Him. The guests needed more wine, and it was delivered right on time. This moment is remembered as Jesus' first miracle.

Yes, Jesus is God, but on the earth, He was both God and man. We have to consider the story found in Luke Chapter 2 specifically dealing with Jesus' response to His earthly parents when they went looking for Him. The conversation in Luke 2:49-51 goes like this:

> Why were you searching for me?" he asked. "Didn't you know I had to be in my Father's house?" But they did not understand what he was saying to them. Then he went down to Nazareth with them and was obedient to them. But his mother treasured all these things in her heart. And Jesus grew in wisdom and stature, and in favor with God and man.

Even at twelve years old, Jesus recognized who His Father was: God in heaven. What stood out here is verse 51: "Then he went down to Nazareth with them and was obedient to them." This stood out because it shows us that Jesus, who was God and man, lived as an example for all of us even in the flesh. In His human form, He had some growing up to do and could not just walk away as He pleased. Though He felt He could, His parents did not agree. The preceding verse informs us that "Jesus grew in wisdom and stature." The boy Jesus at twelve years old though very much still literally the Son of God had to grow in wisdom and into the man He was at the wedding feast when it was time. One chapter later in Luke 3:1, we learn that

Jesus was baptized and His ministry began. Yes, Jesus is aware of the time and being God exists outside of it, but at twelve years old He was getting so much attention because of His wisdom and understanding of the Word. The law would have had lots of attention on Him before it was actually time.

When we read of Jesus' ministry, we see example after example where He had to escape the crowd or the people who planned to destroy Him. What would it have looked like if this had taken place when He was twelve years old? I don't know. But what we do know is that His ministry didn't begin until he was 30 years old (Luke 3:1).

Such an example also sheds light on the importance of surrounding ourselves with wise and supportive mentors and elders. They can see things in us we do not always see in ourselves. That being said, we cannot leave room for just anyone to speak into our lives. We should look to those who are in the Word and who seek God for understanding as opposed to their own wisdom.

When I consider why I delay an assignment, I see that one of my excuses is that the time isn't right. So when I read that Jesus says His "hour has not yet come," I can't help but consider that sometimes I worry about when the right time is and if there is a right time for any of the assignments I have to complete. Timing is important; therefore, we should be prayerful and attentive to when God says it is time to go or wait. But as soon as God says go and everything is aligned on the earth as it is in heaven, we should not hold back wondering if we are ready when He says it is time.

When history was in the making, those involved were not considering if it was the right time or if people were ready for change. When things lined up, whether they felt ready or not, they moved. The choices we make today can create stories that are told over and over again for generations. The wine Jesus made was better than the wine they'd been drinking all night. It was so good the groom shockingly turned to his bride stating they had saved the best of the wine for the last moment. The wine could have run out earlier in the wedding festivities, but it didn't. It did so toward the end. Turns out that was the best time—the right time for Jesus' first miracle, when people least expected it.

I challenge you not to hit the snooze button. Press on! Be obedient to the assignment and watch amazing things come out of it. When God says go, be prepared for the results of your obedience.

In my own experience, there came a point in my walk when I stopped hitting the snooze button, but I also wasn't making any moves. No longer was I confined to my comfort in delay. Instead, I entered something close to panic and similar to feelings of anxiety. This was due to the looming deadline written across the sky reminding me of my assignments.

It reminds me of that feeling I got every time I had a big paper due. I would stay up all night because it had to get done. Still, I managed to procrastinate until six in the morning with two hours left on the clock. Then, when it got to six in the morning that panic would hit me or I would have an adrenaline rush and finish my paper with fifteen minutes to spare. To top off the procrastination, I would hand in the assignment and sleep through the class period without even making an effort to find an excuse for missing class. Can you relate? Or was this just me for all four years of college? Either way, let's get back to the point.

The deadline is like a reminder above our heads that we don't like to acknowledge until we're dangerously close to missing it. It can be a personal deadline or one that involves our relationships.

For example, it felt like yesterday when God told me to apologize to someone I felt had hurt me, but didn't. In my ignorance, I hurt that person. For weeks, I remember fighting with God about this assignment. I gave every excuse in the book. I would explain to God that it was better we kept our distance and no longer remain friends.

I would tell God I was a loner, and I could do me with just Him. I didn't need anyone else.

For the longest, I fought back because I thought I would lose my sanity. But truthfully, it was insane of me to hold on to the opposite of what God wanted from me. I fought because I didn't want to humble myself to do something I didn't think was necessary. I fought back because the clock was ticking, and I knew I was getting dangerously close to missing my deadline. My alarm was blaring, and I just couldn't take it anymore. The places that were once comfortable, that had become my refuge I wanted to avoid.

Unfortunately, or fortunately depending on which side of the coin you're looking at, I was in double jeopardy. I had to be in that place where I was uncomfortable because I was assigned to the room. But being assigned to the room meant I was in close proximity to something else God was asking me to do. For example, if I am called to be in a classroom so I can receive credit for attendance and participation but did not do the assigned homework, I would feel uncomfortable sitting in front of the teacher. Sometimes we avoid the classroom because we did not complete the homework assignment.

If I was obedient to one, I would still be uncomfortable because I ignored the other deadline. If I was disobedient to the place, I would miss my opportunity to be obedient to the assignment. So, day in and day out, weekend after weekend, in my bedroom, in the car driving long distances, stuck in the middle of traffic, I spoke; I screamed; I fought back with God, hitting snooze over and over again until the deadline came. At some point, I knew I had run out of time and could no longer continue to fight. So, I stopped and listened to what God had to say.

I don't know what my life would look like today if I had missed the deadline. I don't know and I don't think I ever need to find out. It doesn't make sense for me to ponder on a decision I didn't make and a deadline I didn't miss. Even in that moment, I knew how important it was that I think ahead and continue to move forward. I decided to obey and be completely reliant on God's strength in me. I had no regrets about my decision. In fact, I slept well that night after weeks of hitting snooze.

To be honest, my breakthrough didn't come because I made a decision to comply. It came because God kept me as noted in Psalm 121. God knew the plans He had for me and would not let me go as long as I was willing to fight.

I am now living in the aftermath of meeting my deadline. The refuge turned arena became a safe haven, which is now my training ground. God is using that space to grow me in ways I could never imagine. I believe He would have done it anyway because I surrendered my all to Him. But sometimes victory depends on our choices and when we choose to surrender. As written in Isaiah 25:1, God's plans for us were laid out a long time ago. Surrendering to His plan will always bear fruit and bring us peace even when it puts us in the middle of a storm. But even surrender requires a response. We get better and better when we've practiced and disciplined ourselves.

Discipline vs. Intentionality

As easy as it is to tell you to wake up when your alarm goes off, it's actually harder to do it. It takes serious discipline, especially when we don't want to be rushed. We set the alarm because we intend to wake up, but when the alarm rings, we wish we had set it back another thirty minutes.

To start, intentionality and discipline cannot play on the same field. They are two different states of mind. One is the aspiration to fulfill something and the other is the straight-up execution of that aspiration. So, our intentions to accomplish our goals and live as God asks is great. However, it means nothing without self-control or discipline. We know self-control is an important characteristic because it is a fruit of the Spirit. To me, this means that without the Holy Spirit, it can be hard to do all God wants us to do.

You may be wondering what we have to do to execute our intentions. The answer is to obey. Intentionality plus obedience results in discipline. A heart obedient to God's instruction can bear fruits of self-control whereas had it been left up to how we feel, the task would not be completed at the appropriate time.

We find in the books of Exodus and Jeremiah, as well as throughout scripture, that God asks us simply to obey. Look at all the Israelites went through from their four hundred years of slavery to the exodus. I imagine this nation in the middle of nowhere as they ate manna from heaven had every intention to obey God's commands. He told them to go out and gather food enough for the day. On the sixth day, they were to gather enough for that day and the next, which was the Sabbath to be honored. So, every day, they would go out to gather bread. However, because they did not trust that God would provide, the Israelites gathered more than a day's portion. When they awoke, the excess food they had gathered had rotted. Quick sidebar— isn't it interesting how we disobey because we do not trust the Commander's best intentions for us? How has our refusal to obey caused the things around us to rot or expire?

This Israelites' gathering of more food than they were instructed is a clear example of intention without obedience. Over and over, they told God they would obey Him. I am sure this intention came from their hearts as they saw the mountain before them tremble with God's presence. Yet, because they did not understand the value of obedience, their intention could not reveal discipline.

All that aside, I think the story of the Israelites in the desert shows the longest period anyone has ever clicked the snooze button.

Let's break it down:

1. The assignment was to get to Canaan, the Promised Land.
2. The alarm was set for 11 days assuming the nation complied.

3. The snooze button was hit every time they disobeyed, lost trust in God, lost faith in his vessel Moses, complained, and forgot who brought them out of slavery.

4. They finally stopped hitting snooze 40 years later, a whole generation of people dead and 39.969883 years late.

I hope I've made my point. It's ridiculous! Yet, we do this to ourselves every day. God wants to bring us to a particular place, and it requires that we trust Him at His word. We are stubborn and stuck in our habits, comfort, and sinful patterns. We complain and want to make our own paths. Thus, we delay His promises in our lives.

When we don't get it right, we place that burden on our children. Living with a snooze button so close to our bed causes life to go by us. It is not okay to make our beds our home all because we do not have discipline. As amazing as our beds are, we have dreams for a life far beyond them. Yet, lack of discipline has made our beds our crutches. Instead of running from the things that disable us, we lean on them to get through life. I urge you to wake up if you're still sleeping. Do not disable yourself for the sake of growing comfortable in something that is supposed to serve a temporary and limited purpose.

Is it going to be easy? Absolutely not. Even Hebrews 12:11 admits that "No discipline seems pleasant at the time, but painful. Later on, however, it produces a harvest of righteousness and peace for those who have been trained by it."

My friend, your training begins now. The alarm has been set. You have free will to hit your snooze button. And yes, God is so gracious He forgives daily and gives us another chance. But remember that you and I do not know the day or the hour. Do not miss the deadline because you have no self-control.

Living My Best Life – ACT II

I want to leave you with a few tips that work for me when I want to be motivated and remain disciplined in my life.

Step 1: *Set your alarm and place it somewhere far away from you.* I mean this literally. If part of completing your assignment means you have to get up at the time you set your alarm to go off, I suggest plugging whatever alarm you use into an outlet on the other side of the room. This way you must register the alarm ringing and get up to silence it.

Surround yourself with living and walking reminders. Who can you trust to follow-up on a deadline? Tell them about your goals. Give them the deadline you need to meet your goals. Check in with them at pre-selected times to share progress updates. Your accountability partner should not be the friend who isn't good at being accountable in his life. If he is lenient with himself, he will likely be lenient with you. He won't check on you or care if you miss your deadline. Think of it as clocking in at work versus not having to clock-in at work. Knowing that the computer keeps you accountable for coming in on time, you arrive to work a little ahead. On the flip side, if you work where no one cares what time you come in, then you're more likely to get there a little late. Remember once you've built a habit of lateness, it becomes hard to undo.

Step 2: *Read the Word.* There is nothing like being reprimanded by God's Word. Perhaps, its ability to almost snap your head and your heart back to attention is the reason why they call it the Living Word. It has me feeling guilty and grateful at the same time. Guilty for forgetting the importance of the assignment but grateful God is forgiving and gracious enough to give me another chance to breathe and get it right the next time around. This reminds me of the song "Be the Place" by Naomi Raine where she said, "We honor you, not just with our lips but with our hearts," which I assume is based on what God says in Matthew 15:8, "These people honor me with their lips, but their hearts are far from me." Decide to honor God, not just with your lips but with your heart. It also reminds me of "My Worship" by Phil Thompson. A verse of the song said, "I will not be silent. I will always worship you." Worship is not just something we do in a song or with our lips. Worship is a lifestyle.

Step 3: *Create a routine.* My weekday routine is different from my weekend routine. My weekday routine is pretty consistent. Mondays through Fridays look the same for me. Keep your to-do list to the minimum when you first wake up so you can be consistent with it. It is helpful to build discipline by starting small.

Step 4: *Surround yourself with like-minded people.* I touched on this in step two relating to choosing my accountability partners. But in this step, I'm talking about your friends and mentors. Who is in your ear and has influence in your life? Surrounding yourself with like-minded people is important because their approach to life and day-to-day attitude will affect your life and attitude. For example, let's say you have a daily unscheduled call with your best friend. She has a habit of putting her work aside, choosing ice-cream and pasta over fruits and veggies, or watching television instead of meeting a work deadline. If you are not careful, you will find yourself mimicking her behavior. So be picky about who you are giving your time to and when you are giving it to them.

CHAPTER 7:

HIDING PLACE

I think that as soon as I grew into the hiding place, it became one of my favorite spots. Many of us have that favorite place in our houses or favorite spots in a room. My hiding place with God is similar. It is one of the places that feels just right. The hiding place, the secret place, the prayer room, prayer closet, the war room and so many terms like these have been used interchangeably to refer to the place where we go to meet with God. In the movie "War Room" with Priscilla Shirer, the war room is emphasized as the place all believers can find rest.

Protection & Deliverance

When we look at Scripture, we find that David refers to his time spent with God as his hiding place. In Psalm 32:7 specifically, he said, "You are my hiding place; you will protect me from trouble and surround me with songs of deliverance." This tells us that in this place with God, we are protected and delivered from trouble. It doesn't mean that trouble no longer surrounds us, it just means that we've been delivered out of the burden that trouble brings.

At first read, protection and deliverance from trouble may seem common. Yet, I tell you that there are many things even now that God is protecting you from. No matter the country we are citizen to and no matter the city in which we reside, know that there is no house, no locked door, no security alarm, or bullet-proof window that can protect and deliver us from trouble. You see, trouble is not picky about who or how it attacks. Trouble appears physically, emotionally, mentally, and spiritually.

A locked house can be locked until someone with adequate skills comes along and unlocks it. A security alarm can be set in every nook, window, and door in your house, but it cannot physically stop someone from coming into your space. A bulletproof window, no matter how seemingly impenetrable, shatters after being hit repeatedly.

But David tells us in the psalms what many of us have discovered for ourselves: protection and deliverance are in the hiding place. Romans 8:31 reminds us that "If God is for us then who can be against us?" When we call on the name of Jesus, we are asking for a level of protection and deliverance that we can't even afford but have access to because of relationship. All of that said, a believer's greatest peace is in knowing that even if they lose their lives, they have gained eternity with Christ. To this fact, we know that the weapon will be formed and used against us but even as we stare down the chamber of the bullet, it will not prosper.

This means so many things to so many people. Some will end up unscathed. Look at the story found in Acts 14:19 about when Paul was stoned and how he got up and went about his day as if he wasn't supposed to be dead. Or we can refer to the story of Daniel in the lion's den in Daniel 6:16. No, let's consider Daniel and his friends when they were thrown into a furnace and walked out without the smell of smoke on their clothes in Daniel 3:26-27. For others, this could mean the bullet will penetrate. Paul was beaten and imprisoned in Acts 16:22-24. The bullet will not kill or stop you similar to when Paul was bitten by a snake and kept it pushing in Acts 28:3-6.

As mentioned previously, death is not what we, as believers, should be afraid of. Even when the Enemy thinks he's taken our joy from us, may we keep standing knowing that joy comes in the morning. It is bittersweet; I am sure, but there is life after this! A level of peace comes with the protection and deliverance attached to the Lord and being in the hiding place with Him.

God's Presence, Protection, and Promotion

Now you're probably curious to know how to get in this hiding place. As excited as you are, I want to first let you know what you can expect to find there. I want to highlight that in the hiding place, we find God's presence, protection, and promise, and promotion. If we look at Psalm 27:5, we will find God's presence, protection, and promotion: "For in the day of trouble, he will keep me safe in his dwelling; he will hide me in the shelter of his sacred tent and set me high upon a rock." Let's break it down.

God's Presence

The psalmist notes that in "his dwelling" or in God's dwelling, which we can interpret as God's presence, we find safety. To dwell is to live in a specified place. God asks that we live in or dwell in Him. How do we know this to be true? When we look at John 15:3-4, we find that over and over again God asks us to remain in Him and His love, so His Word would remain in us. This will certainly help us to bear fruit beyond what we could bear outside of His presence.

The hiding place is one of our spiritual defenses. Your hiding place can be a physical space or mindset. I highly recommend that you assign a space spiritually or physically to meet God for yourself. We can seek His presence daily, but every day comes with its own distractions. The biggest difference between life and your hiding place is that you will go about your life anyway, but a purposeful decision is necessary to dwell in God's presence.

When we are intentional about seeking God in our lives, we create a space where we can prioritize Him. There is something about seeking God as my priority that brings a level of prayer I didn't know existed in me—a level of fight I didn't lift weights to qualify for, and a level of peace and understanding that comes from the One who knows everything.

When we dwell in God's presence, we fill that dwelling with worship and praise, prayer and conversation, quiet and submission, discipline, and repentance. We are to seek God fervently desiring to be at His feet, hear His voice, and trust Him with all our troubles. One thing I enjoy about my hiding place is that God places things and people in my heart to pray for and situations to pray against.

In the book of Exodus, the scripture notes moments when God asks Moses to remove himself from the people, distractions, and food to come into His presence. God instructed Moses to go to the top of the mountain alone and away from it all. There is nowhere we can go without God. He is always speaking and if we are willing to hear Him, even as a whisper in a crowd of people, we will hear Him clearly. But I believe God blesses intentionality. When we seek God on purpose, He is always there waiting for us. I am not positive I can explain God's omniscience in a clear and edifying way but when we speak to and hear from God, we can do so through the Holy Spirit.

Who is the Holy Spirit? If we turn to 2 Corinthians 3:17, we learn, "Now the Lord is the Spirit, and where the Spirit of the Lord is, there is freedom." In John 14:16-17, Jesus tells His disciples:

> *And I will ask the Father, and he will give you another advocate to help you and be with you forever— the Spirit of truth. The world cannot accept him, because it neither sees him nor knows him. But you know him, for he lives with you and will be in you.*

The Spirit of truth is also referred to as the Holy Spirit or the Holy Ghost. Jesus tells us in John Chapter 14 how the Holy Spirit lives in those who accept Him (Jesus). The Holy Spirit will be with us. Hence, if we do not accept Jesus Christ as our Lord, we cannot accept or know the Holy Spirit. This is confirmed in 1 Corinthians 12:3 where Paul writes, "Therefore I want you to know that no one who is speaking by the Spirit of God says, 'Jesus be cursed,' and no one can say, 'Jesus is Lord,' except by the Holy Spirit."

But still, who is the Holy Spirit? The Holy Spirit is God's Spirit. John 15:26 reads, "When the Advocate comes, whom I will send to you from the Father—the Spirit of truth who goes out from the Father—he will testify about me." So not only is the Holy Spirit God's Spirit but when we accept Jesus Christ as our Lord and Savior, we can then accept and know God's Spirit. Again, when we look at 1

John 4:4, as believers, we are confident knowing He who is in us is greater than he who is in the world. I say all this to say God in the form of His Spirit lives within us; thus, He is with us wherever we go. When we are led to pray, when we hear from and talk to God, it is with His Spirit that we communicate. When we feel a nudge to do the righteous thing, not because we want to but because something in us encourages us to, then know outrightly it is the Holy Spirit. In the same way, the Holy Spirit advocates on our behalf as we understand from Romans 8:26: "In the same way, the Spirit helps us in our weakness. We do not know what we ought to pray for, but the Spirit himself intercedes for us through wordless groans."

God did not live inside of sinful people before Jesus' sacrifice. We will have a better understanding when we read Psalm 27:5.

God's Protection

The psalmist says, "He will hide me in the shelter of his sacred tent." This means covering and shelter are in His sacred tent. The sacred tent in some Bible versions is also called the tabernacle. We understand the tabernacle as a holy place where God dwells among His people. Note that God dwelled among His people in this sacred tent and in this consecrated space, but He did not live in them as He lives in us. We are now temples for the Lord. The sacred tent or tabernacle is consecrated, made holy and dedicated for God to dwell in. God asks the same from us as His temples.

In reference to the "sacred tent," God instructed Moses and the Israelites how they should build the dwelling, but do not misunderstand this to mean He was not with them outside of it.

Please know that hiding in God's shelter does not excuse cowardice. To hide is to conceal from the view of others. To cower is to hide in fear of something: our calling, assignment, purpose, and gifts. A friend shared with me that we can look at the hiding place as dwelling in God's shadow.

I believe God goes ahead of us in everything. We can see Him working when we give Him the stage, make Him the pilot of our airplanes, the captain of our ships, and the driver of our vehicles. This tells me two things:

1. We must not hide within ourselves because living for God requires that we live boldly
2. God's shadow, His presence, is bigger than that thing we are scared of in the light.

What do I mean by this?

It will be easier for me to explain this if I share from my experience. I have introverted characteristics, and I can cover them up well if I have too. If it is between fight or flight, I will fight. But I've never been the type to always be in front of the camera. I was always behind it and that's where I felt happy and safe.

After a hard season that drew me into the hiding place, God began to remold me and remove every branch that did not bear fruit in me (John 15:2). In this hiding place, He told me I could no longer exist within the thought process I had grown comfortable identifying myself with. I could no longer hide within myself and my excuses. God told me I was not an introvert. That an introvert could not serve Him and even more, be obedient to the assignment.

When I tell you I was torn, I was *torn* beyond repair. I was in a place where I loved God more than I could ever grasp in my hands, much less in my heart. But here He was telling me if I truly loved Him I would let go of my comfort to be obedient to the call He predestined for my life. I was torn because I really believed I was an introvert. To top it, I was certain that was how God designed and expected me to live my life. I thought He arranged it so that I would serve according to my introverted characteristics: behind the scenes and undercover.

I equated hiding with protection, but as God revealed to me who I really was, I understood I was nothing more than a coward.

What I didn't understand initially but know now was that before God formed me, He knew me, and then He formed me in my mother's womb (Jeremiah 1:5). He who formed me designed me in His likeness and gave me everything I needed to serve Him in obedience (2 Peter 1:3). For too long, I hid within myself and was comforted by who the world told me I was. Unfortunately, I accepted it as the truth because it made me feel comfortable.

With all of that said and done, there came a morning when I had to lead a song before my peers and my elders. When I tell you I was not okay—I was not okay. Over and over again, I prayed and rehearsed until I became comfortable enough to hold the microphone and open my mouth to sing. Even as I sang, I felt as if I wanted to recede within. But knowing there was nowhere left for me to go but forward, I closed my eyes and sought the Lord in the same hiding place.

As I sang, I felt a confidence that didn't come from anything I could ever exercise just working in me. When I opened my eyes, I was no longer afraid. Instead, I was surrounded by my brothers and sisters who were also moved by the Holy Spirit that had erupted in me. The Lord is my strength and my hiding place. They were moved by my obedience because I chose to hide in the shadow of my God. I remember crying in my sisters' arms afterward as they cried in mine. It touched me to hear them say they were so proud of me, not because I sang well but because I had surrendered my comfort to be obedient. Sometimes God calls us to places, people, and spaces where our comfort is in a tug-of-war with our obedience. It was then that I understood what it felt like to hide in God's shadow. It wasn't me in front of people. In fact, it wasn't about the people. I was singing for an audience of one and my job was to lead them into His presence.

I am a vessel created to do all God made me to do. We are all vessels predestined to live lives that are pleasing to God. Our hearts have to agree. Jesus will spit out lukewarm people from His mouth because He doesn't want half of us; He wants all of us.

From that day on, I decided to make a conscious effort to choose God first and erase the fear in me. I don't want to live out my life as a coward. Does this mean my introverted nature just flew out the door? The short answer is yes and no. I have introverted characteristics but when it comes to all that God has asked me to do, they get kicked out of the room. My cowardice cannot sit at the table with God's calling on my life. One thing I did, especially at the beginning of this season, was to pray before I said no. I learned to accept every invitation where God gave me peace. I don't mean the subsiding of palpitations that were taking place in my heart, but the peace that comes with knowing He is with me and will continue to be my hiding place.

God will catch us when we fall. He is our protection when we are vulnerable, and His eyes see everything, even as we close our own. Know also that there is power in you. It is a power you have not even begun to touch. Continue to obey and hide in Him. Be intentional about dwelling in His presence.

To continue, the hiding place not only pulls things out of us but it protects us from external things as well. For example, we are protected from the critiques of our peers. Sometimes the people who love us and even those who dislike us will say things to trigger a memory or lack within us. While the hiding place does not stop people from trying to tear us down, it will be like a fortified wall that is unable to collapse because we know what God told us. Remember, I wanted to be a lawyer, but God said no. Every now and then, someone with a word of critique will look at me, my life, and my potential and ask me why I wasn't already in law or graduate school. These were innocent questions until I got tired of having to explain myself to the same people who didn't get it. It took some time to be okay with what

God told me and to put that as precedence over what others said about me. God has something else in store for me, and I trust Him. His Word is protection from the critiques and thoughts of others about how we should lead our lives.

God's Promotion

Additionally, the hiding place protects us from promotion that does not belong to us. I know it sounds crazy, who doesn't want a promotion? Everyone wants a promotion, but not every promotion is for you. This means that at times, you will have to say no. The hiding place is not only for when you're going through tough times, but also when things are looking up for you. Seek God for direction in everything because moving forward without His approval is like taking a bet on you and your ability.

Let's pretend you accept the work promotion because you hope it'll improve your life. With the promotion comes higher pay, additional responsibility, and longer hours. The paychecks are bigger, but now you have to sacrifice the time you had to prior commitments, including ministry and your family just to name a couple of things. Trying to obtain some semblance of control and order in your life, you begin a balancing act between work, ministry, and family. You are overwhelmed and probably don't even know it. Why haven't you realized your fatigue? It is because while trying to give all of yourself to what you consider priorities: work, ministry, and family, you forgot something very important. That is, to pour into these areas of your life, you need to spend time alone with God. If you don't do that, before you know it, you will be burned out. You will want to climb to the top of a mountain until you feel ready to face the world again.

Anything that pulls you away from your assignment wreaks havoc in other areas of your life that are supposed to be spaces that bring you peace. This may be hard to totally understand but not everything that looks like a step forward is one. It is a step back if it is not in God's plan for you. The Enemy is great at disguising a distraction as a blessing. Check the Holy Spirit for everything. As Proverbs 3:5-6 tells us, "Trust in the Lord with all your heart, lean not on your own understanding, but in all your ways acknowledge him and he will direct your path."

Promotion also goes hand-in-hand with exposure. For example, with promotion, your lack of self-discipline will be exposed. With promotion, your harsh tongue and language will be open for all to see and hear. With promotion, even disorder within your family is open for others to judge and critique. Your title is not the only thing that changes; it is like replacing the walls of your house with see-through glass. What you do, who you are, and how you live in private are all reflected in the public eye vulnerable to critique and expectation.

You see, when you said yes to promotion, you thought you were only saying yes to a larger salary and perhaps extra working hours. But in the fine lines of every contract for promotion is your consent for people to look at you, expect things of you, judge you, and speak about you as if they know every single detail of your life. When you are not firmly established and solid about who you are and the spaces God has called you to, you are like a brick wall that was never glued together. With every hammer to your character, the house that represents you begins to crumble. Secure the walls before you invite people in and make sure God is the one holding everything together because you aren't strong enough. We are weak, vulnerable, fatigued human beings. We are not strong enough to carry the expectations of the world on our shoulders.

Be Who God Designed You to Be

Further, the hiding place gives you the strength to love, forgive, and be patient in every season you are overlooked in. In this place, focus on who God is saying you are and not who everyone else is pretending to be. Yes, I said it because some of us have taken several steps too far away from who we are to be accepted by others. Changing this culture of comparison has to start with you.

If we focus on ourselves and grow into who God sees when He looks at us, we will be happier. Moreover, we will be able to congratulate the strides being made by others without resentment, contempt, or jealousy. On the other hand, sometimes it seems people just don't see us, refuse to acknowledge our gifts and our talents, and intentionally pick us last for the team. Do not worry about what people see when they look at you or what they don't see.

There is a purpose and lesson in every season you were overlooked. Sometimes you are overlooked because as ready as you may think you are, God wants to change a few more things in you. These same things will better help you manage the next season well. Exposure is a real thing.

Let's say you've been training to be a worship leader. You've been drinking your water and doing voice exercises, but you don't know what it means to worship, how can you lead others into worship? How will you avoid taking God's glory for yourself? Afterall, it is easier to steal from someone you do not know. If you are acknowledged in this season, but you do not know God, when you sing and the crowd claps, you will mistake His praise and credit it to your gifting. To avoid the downfall that would inevitably follow, God hides us to prune us, to cleanse us, and teach us.

Sometimes it is for our future wellbeing that we are overlooked in the present. We are to be rooted so deep in God that even a tornado cannot stop us from rising up again. In these seasons of growing, we are at our most fragile. We are vulnerable to the critique of those around us, we are also vulnerable to the opinions and well-meant suggestions of those who have influence over us. But God wants us to grow with Him so that we can stand strong and immoveable when the winds blow, and the waves come. God plants us beneath the soil so that when we sprout, we will have a solid foundation. There is covering and preparation in God's shadow.

Further, sometimes we are overlooked because God wants to bring us to a place that others cannot follow. If we are noticed by those who cannot go where God wants to take us, we might drag along baggage we have no business carrying into a new season with its new revelations and challenges. As the psalmist says in Psalm 27:5, God has "set [us] high upon a rock" and that rock was designed to carry a certain load. Therefore, when we slip and feel defeated let's take it as an opportunity to evaluate our circle. Being defeated doesn't always say something about how well you fight, but rather if you are surrounded by people who will fight with you.

This is not to say you should not care, love, and support those who were with you from the beginning. It is simply that something different is required of you in every season and too many voices can cause you to falter. For example, if in every new season you continue to carry along that friend who thinks the same as in high school, while your mind has been transformed and renewed, then you had better think again.

Very quick sidebar—this is why it is so important to be equally yoked with your wife or husband. This is why it is so important to continue to read, grow, and date while in a marital relationship. Your mind should not be what it was when you first got married. It should be elevated, filled, and matured with the revelation and wisdom God gives you; wisdom born out of experience, knowledge, and God's truth. There is purpose in marriage. Marriage was not the purpose; it was just the next stop to your ultimate destination. The difference between a longtime friendship and a marriage is that where you go, your spouse goes. In these moments, the question can no longer be, "Who is going with me?" and "Who is on my team?" The statement must be, "God, I see you moving; prepare me for wherever you want to take me." The same rules apply to singles. Everyone you date or are interested in is not meant to be your husband or wife. Stop dragging extra people along to be a part of the journey.

In a conversation with a friend, they suggested that sometimes we are overlooked because God wants to preserve us. This made me think of the china set example we used earlier. One set of utensils is more reserved and set apart for special occasions. In the same way, we are overlooked as a form of preservation. As I reflected on this, I realized that those who are preserved are also marked. Those who are marked are also called, chosen, sealed, predestined, and saved (Romans 8:30). All of these are names God has given His people. God calls us friends, heirs, and a royal priesthood. All of these names describe something or someone who is set apart. When we look at ourselves and understand we are set apart because God wants to preserve us, we no longer feel pressed to be a part of everything everyone else is involved in. Fear of missing out on an opportunity is no longer an issue.

In Psalm 27:5, we uncover some meaning in the verse that says, "Set me high upon a rock." What is a rock if not something elevated and set apart? Think about it—soil and cement are level ground. On a freezing cold day, there is no distinction between the two. If you were to walk along a path with your eyes closed, you wouldn't know which of the two your feet are walking across. However, the minute your foot lands on a rock, you know it. It hurts a lot because your foot is elevated in one area, while the weight of your body pushes down on the remaining and un-elevated part as you attempt to take another step. In the same way, when David explains how God "set me high upon a rock," we see promotion and pain. I don't think it means literal pain, but the pain that comes from isolation and being disconnected from the familiar. The root word of "promote" is "meue," which means to push away. Like how the moment I jump on one corner of a trampoline, the person on the other side would be sent up and away from me.

Bringing It Together

I think Noah's story is a great example of the three components of the hiding place: presence, protection, and promotion. In Genesis Chapter 6, we learn that Noah was among the first people God created. In verse 13, we find that God instructed Noah to build an ark in anticipation of a great flood that would destroy everything on the earth. Over some time, Noah built the ark and in following God's specific instructions, he welcomed two of every animal: male and female to enter the security of the ark. In Genesis 8:4, we learn that after the rain stopped pouring and on the seventeenth day and seventh month, the ark landed on the top of a mountain. God then gave Noah and his family permission to leave it and walk on the earth again. Noah and his family were saved and protected from the catastrophe brought on by the great flood because there was a relationship. A relationship with God is more than an "I don't know about you, but I'm saved" mentality. It is more of an "I walk with God day by day. He hears me, and I obey Him." Noah had a relationship with God. When they came out of the ark, they found that they had landed atop a mountain. I can't help but connect this to what is written in Psalm 27:5, which tells us that "God set me high upon a rock." This verse tells me that we can see God's presence and God's protection when we look back at all He brought us through.

Whether we are familiar with the meaning behind the symbol of God's promise or not, God kept His word to Noah concerning the flood that destroyed the earth and everything that was in it. In Genesis 9:13-15, God told Noah,

I have set my rainbow in the clouds, and it will be the sign of the covenant between me and the earth. Whenever I bring clouds over the earth and the rainbow appears in the clouds, I will remember my covenant between me and you and all living creatures of every

kind. Never again will the waters become a flood to destroy all life.

While God promised that He would not judge the earth with water again, we learn in 2 Peter 3:7 that the "heavens and the earth are reserved for fire" on the day of judgment. God protected all who were His when He sent the flood. In the same way, God patiently waits for us to choose Him, to be in His presence, in His protection, and to have hope for His promises on the day of judgment. He does not want us to perish (2 Peter 3:9). In summary, let us make the Lord our hiding place and seek Him earnestly so we may hear when He says, "Go."

Now that we recognize the importance of making the Lord our hiding place and what comes with it, this question remains: how do we get there?

Firstly, a relationship with our heavenly Father is a life-or-death matter. In John 14:6, the first step is laid out plainly for us to understand. The scripture reads:

> *Thomas said to him, "Lord, we don't know where you are going, so how can we know the way?" Jesus answered, "I am the way and the truth and the life. No one comes to the Father except through me.*

In order to get to Jesus we must accept the salvation He offers us. In Romans 10:9-10, we discover how we will be saved. The scripture reads,

> *If you declare with your mouth, "Jesus is Lord," and believe in your heart that God raised him from the dead, you will be saved. For it is with your heart that you believe and are justified, and it is with your mouth that you profess your faith and are saved.*

I know this isn't the typical church, and there isn't a tangible altar to walk to. But for my brothers and sisters to whom these words of Christ belong, please hear what Jesus says to you. Answer your doors and welcome Him as He knocks and be saved (Revelation 3:20). Do not perish for the sake of people or culture. Do not perish because you "haven't arrived," "aren't clean enough for church folk," or "don't know enough about Jesus." I was about eleven or twelve years old when I was saved. It was at a summer camp held in the lower level of my church for kids varied in age. In the space of a week, I learned everything I needed to know at the time. That is, Jesus knew me, He loved me more than I could ever and will ever grasp in my then smaller hands and even my fully grown hands now. To top it, He wanted to be my friend.

Perhaps, it was easier for me to believe because I was a child (Matthew 19:14). But now, I'm grown up, and every single day I am confounded and bombarded by the way God has revealed Himself to me over and over again. I have even more reason to say yes to Jesus today than ever before and still what little I knew in the beginning was enough. He says the same things to you. Jesus knew you before you were in your mother's womb (Jeremiah 1:5). He loves you more than you could ever imagine even with every new day and season, and He wants to be your friend—in spite of yourself. Isn't that amazing! There are things that we would never tell people, but Jesus already knows about every little secret and still He invites us into His presence. Jesus isn't holding back, neither should you. This thought brings me to tears.

But back to how we can get to the hiding place. When we are saved in Jesus, we have access to the Father. God is a good Father in so many ways and He wants us, His children, to seek Him. We can reach the hiding place by getting to know Him and interacting with Him through His Word, worship, praise, and prayer.

It is critical that we make time in our daily routines to get to know our heavenly Father. This makes it sound like we are prioritizing our lives above our time with God, but that's not the case. When we set our appointments according to our daily routine, we can be sure to set uninterrupted time for God.

Outside of location, time, and consistency, our hearts and the spirit behind seeking the hiding place is what makes it a hiding place. It is a place where we are honest, no forms of pretense. It is a place where we find God and hear from Him. It is a place where we repeatedly submit our control, plans, weaknesses, and innate characteristics to Him to do whatever He pleases.

I have enjoyed seeking God through His Word, prayer, and song when walking, for example, from the train station to my house. I've also enjoyed seeking Him while in my car in the middle of traffic. As my life changed, I was able to find spaces where I could seek God and sit with Him. My favorite place to seek Him now is on my walks. I enjoy seeing His glory and the creation of His hands while I talk with Him. Additionally, it doesn't matter if the time you can sacrifice and give to God is at five in the morning or eleven at night. But the time with God is sacred and necessary if we are to accomplish anything in life. I find that I can't even manage my basic responsibilities without spending designated time with God.

Living My Best Life – ACT III

Here are a couple of recommendations that have worked for me to get into the hiding place. Remember to consider your reality and permit it to make sense for you. I'm only one person and can't speak for everyone, but I hope these help point you in the right direction.

Step 1: I highly recommend that your hiding place be somewhere secluded where no one can find you or where the people around you know not to bother you at that time. In my household, there is this mood my parents switch into when entering their hiding place that transforms the basement or living room into a church. From years of watching their patterns and being reminded of what it meant for them to meet with God, we learned not to bother them. That being said, I don't have any children and no one depends on me to be okay, so time in the hiding place will be different for me as it is for everyone. You may not be able to hide from a toddler for twenty minutes, much less for a bathroom break. In such a case, you would have to be intentional in seeking God throughout your day and setting sacrificial time out to meet with Him.

Step 2: This next recommendation is a big one for me because of how easy it is for me to get distracted. Being distraction-free is key. Television is distracting to me when I have work to do, but I can fold laundry while having a conversation. I have had to stay at home many times because the weather outside was distracting: too cold, too hot, or rainy. So while inside, I usually place a scarf over my head to help me focus on my time with God.

Placing the scarf on my head does two things. Firstly, when I cover my head, I cut off distractions from the world around me. I go from vertical living, seeing what is around me, to a horizontal relationship—closing off what is around me to focus on God who is above me. Its second responsibility falls along the same lines. It cuts off people and things that aren't invited into that conversation. Obviously, a scarf doesn't give off sound but just like headphones, it signals you want to be left alone.

I'm excited for the transformation that will take place in your life after you've discovered your hiding place. Get ready for a change in perspective, a clear mind and instructions, as well as a heart that beats more and more for God every day.

CHAPTER 8:

GOD'S FINISHED WORD

Dear God,

> *Jesus at the center of it all*
> *Jesus at the center of it all*
> *From beginning to the end*
> *It will always be, it's always been You Jesus*
> *Jesus*
> *Nothing else matters, nothing in this world will do*
> *Jesus You're the center, and everything revolves around You*
> *Jesus You*
> *From my heart to the heavens*
> *Jesus be the center*
> *It's all about you*
> *Yes, it's all about*
>
> *-Israel & New Breed, Decade, 2012*

Dear God, I Can't Do Me Without You is not about me; it is all about Jesus. It is not about what I can do, my skills, and my capacity. It is not about my breath because my heart can't beat without it. It is not about my legs because I can't walk this journey without them. It is not about my voice or my words because you influence them. *Dear God, I Can't Do Me Without You* is about Your finished word not just in my life but our lives.

Let me start from the top, so we can be on the same page. Before I began to write the words in this book, I wrote blogs on my blog site "Ash's Cafe." A majority of those blogs were conceived out of a real-time conversation with God. Weekly, I would seek Him for a word, and faithfully He would give me a message to share. Whether a lot of people were reading, just one person, or even no one at all, what kept me encouraged was how I saw His Word come to life through my own experiences and those of the people around me. He gave me vision and a space where I could draw the picture with my words. I didn't need anyone else to agree on God's Word spoken to me, and that hasn't changed. It was a fine line between knowing a secret before it was revealed, and the vulnerability of having to be the one to do that. The blog disciplined and humbled me.

So fast-forward to the present day of writing this book. I am in actual tears because I do not know how I got to this point. As I sit trying to figure out how to close this chapter, I see what it feels like to have words escape me because of my shock. How did I get to this point? Why me? This is crazy. I don't write books and the books I start to write I never finish. Yet, here I am, attempting to write the last words for this book. I hope I haven't lost you.

....

During the period that led to writing the initial draft to this last chapter, I kept asking God to tell me how to bring it all together. What was the point? Day after day, I brought Chapter 8 before God, and day after day I waited. Finally, God spoke and told me that the spirit behind this book is His finished word in me. At the beginning of the year, God told me one thing and one thing only: this would be the year of fulfilled promises. So you have to understand I was giddy when He shared this with me. I immediately wanted to break out into song as if I was in a musical session.

As excited as I was, God immediately brought me back to present-day reality. He told me that though I was excited about His finished word in this one area, there were other areas where I hesitated. The best way I can think of to explain this to you is to paint the picture a little bit.

God reminded me of the time He told me I would be hired for my first job out of college. Recalling the moment, several things were highlighted. The first was that I believed it when He showed me. The second was that I agreed with what He had shown me, and the third was that I didn't worry about being hired at the job afterward. I lived my life as though His word had already come to pass. I lived as though I was already existing in His finished word.

Then God compared that revelation to a more recent one. Maybe one day, I'll have the opportunity to share that revelation with you, but for now, the only thing you need to know is that God showed me something and I didn't believe Him. He showed me also how I refused to accept the revelation and how I was constantly worried about my interpretation of it. A small part of me understood the revelation; it was clear and simple. But the other part of me started comparing what God revealed to me to what I thought I knew. That's what got me into trouble. I was very focused on the mess I saw and failed to remember that my God was bigger.

I say all this to encourage you to believe God no matter what. Believe the revelation despite the mess you see. Forget where you came from and what you know. Focus straight ahead and not on what took place behind you. The comparison between when I believe God and when I hesitate reminds me of Lot's wife. In Genesis 19:1-23, we learn that God sends angels to destroy Sodom and Gomorrah. Lot and his family were living in a small town near these cities. To cut the long story short, he finds favor with the Lord and the angels warn him to take his family and leave before the time comes for them to destroy it. Lot and his wife were given one instruction: move forward and never look back. I don't know if it was curiosity or disbelief that caused Lot's wife to look back, but the moment she did, she became a pillar of salt. I can't help but draw a connection here to God telling me to stop looking back at my mess and just look forward.

I don't want to be stuck and I don't want you my friend to get stuck in the past either. Instead, press forward, believing, and trusting the revelation God has given you. Go—as we are instructed to do in the Great Commission and watch as His finished word unfolds in our lives. When we dwell on the things and the people behind us, we risk being destroyed by our past, and forfeiting our future. This reveals itself in the form of anxiety, depression, and other stressors that deal with being unable to change or undo what has already been done.

When we dwell on the things and the people behind us, we risk forfeiting the things and the people in front of us. Life is already hard enough, why do we feel the need to carry our sins, mistakes, and missteps while trying to stay afloat in the body of water called life? There are already enough waves coming at us from different directions. But if we keep our eyes fixed on what is before, we will never have to worry about drowning. This is God's grace and mercy. Remember that with growth comes increased responsibility.

We have to pay attention to the details, be flexible enough to change routes, and be calculated enough to take a risk in circumstances where there are no other options. This is why I am so grateful for grace and for the blood of Jesus. He died so that we would not have to carry and pay the ransom for our sins. He died so that we might live and have hope. He died so that we might be set free. Ah, I love it! John 8:36 tells us, "So if the Son set you free, you are free indeed." Even this scripture has a level of choice in it. It is your decision if you choose to look back, but know that if you choose to be set free from your chains, bondage, past and your generational history, then you are free indeed. In Jesus' name. Thank You, Jesus for freedom! Here I am free and eyes fixed on You. I trust You, God. I don't know how I made it to this point, but I trust You.

I can recall when I heard someone say some people have the heart to write and some don't. I sat on that for a long time. I believed I didn't have the heart to write. I'm too easily distracted and as much as I enjoy writing and helping others, I have no personal motivation to sit down and write an entire book. Yet, here I am after many months, writing the last chapter. A heart for writing I might not have, but what I do have is a heart of obedience. That obedience is what brought me to this point, completely overwhelmed and confused about how I finally made it. This is God's finished word in my life— at least, for this chapter of my life. I am so excited to see His glory come through. No matter what, I surrender my life and plans to His way.

I love the way Paul says it over and over again. In so many ways, he says he is a prisoner for Christ. I believe the same thing about myself. I desire to be a prisoner for Jesus because, so help me God, I can't do me, without You!

....

Dear God,

I could never thank You enough. I am not deserving of Your grace, mercy, forgiveness, faithfulness, or patience. Still, You love and chose me. I thank You that You are not a man who would lie. I know Your word never returns to You void. I am reminded of this every day. Thank You for the vision to see that the sun, moon, and stars still obey Your first word to them. Thank You that the heavens remain parted to create Earth and sky. Thank You that the waters have not overtaken the land. Thank You that the authority You established for man to have over all other creation has not changed hands. The first people may have been destroyed but Your word to them, Your word to all of creation in the first seven days of its birth, those words were never destroyed.

Thank You for waiting for me. You waited for me to be able to understand that I don't need to understand. You waited for me to see that I didn't need to see. You waited for me to know that my sight would always fail me. But that my ears, the words You spoke into my life, the promises You whispered into my ears, Your voice—thank You for letting me understand Your voice was all that I needed. Thank You, Jesus, for designing me to do me but never to do it without You. I love You.

God's finished word is our assignment, and the thing that unlocks our ability to complete it is that we "Love the Lord [y]our God with all [y]our heart and with all [y]our soul and with all [y]our mind. This is the first and greatest commandment" (Matthew 22:37).

EPILOGUE

Hey, friend! Do you remember at the start of the book how I lived life according to my introverted nature? That was only one layer God had to remove to reveal all of who I truly am. Here's a little view into something that had to change in me. I pray this will challenge you to take a better look at your life.

To start, I had to quit the job. I had to remove people from my life and embrace temporary isolation because I used those things and people to define who I was. I was looking for my identity in people and in things instead of in my Creator. Jeremiah 1:5 says that God knew me before He formed me. According to Psalm 139:13, He formed me in my mother's womb and in 1 Peter 2:9, God calls me a royal priesthood and His.

Who did I think I was to let people and things decide who they wanted me to be when God Himself created me? As I allowed those things and people to mold me into what they wanted, I was moving farther and farther away from God's plans for me. As a result, I became confused about who I was, what I wanted, and what I believed about myself. I struggled to hear God for myself, so even though I was moving, I wasn't making any progress in His ultimate plan.

Yes, I am grateful for where God has brought me from and into. Every day I have to look to Him for my instruction. Until He returns for us, there is no point at which we can say, "I've arrived." It is so easy to be distracted if not by people or materialistic things, then maybe by fear, procrastination, and feelings of worthlessness. Either way, when we make the decision to change our lives, we don't just impact our future but the lives of the generations to come out of us.

At some point, we have to take a stand and say that the things we went through, no one else, including our children will have to experience.

Let us be free from the pressures and the bondage of this world. Sometimes we struggle with admitting we want to be free because we think the cost is too heavy. While it is difficult because of the battles we will have to face and the trials we may have to overcome, it is still easier to do life with Christ than without Him. The cost of believing in Christ is that we will be free from the world. The cost is that we will have life more abundantly. We will bear fruit we could never carry alone. We will have power over what previously held us captive. There is a way out of the depression you've been living in. There is a way out of the anxiety and worry you've existed with for years. The spirit of loneliness and lack will have to flee because you will know you are never alone. You will know that you are royalty. So lift your head from the ground and look above. Jesus is your way out. John 8:36 says, "For if the Son sets you free, you are free indeed." Period. Thank you Jesus!

This is all great and good. You feel motivated and encouraged, but you may be thinking, what now? Well, now you let go and let God. Now you can declare that depression, anxiety, addiction, laziness, abuse, lying, cheating, faithlessness, and more ends with you. Declare that this is the last season of bondage. Declare that this is the last season you let in the wrong relationships and experiences. Declare in the name of Jesus Christ that it ends with you.

Turn the page. Your children will not have to deal with all you had to deal with. They will not have to repeat and follow in your footsteps. They will not be filled with liquor and drugs but instead with the Holy Spirit who heals and touches all and knows us better than we know ourselves. Declare that it ends with you. In Jesus' name.

At the end of that journey is something you probably never imagined you could possess. It is a thing called freedom. How many of us, knowing how expensive that is, wouldn't want that for our